KT-502-613

25 WALKS

EDINBURGH
AND
LOTHIAN

25 WALKS

EDINBURGH AND LOTHIAN

Roger Smith

Series Editor: Roger Smith

LOTHIAN
REGIONAL COUNCIL

EDINBURGH:HMSO

© Crown copyright 1995

First published 1995

Applications for reproduction should be made to HMSO

Acknowledgements

I am grateful for the willing help given by the councillors and officers of Lothian Regional Council and the Districts of the City of Edinburgh, West Lothian, Midlothian and East Lothian while this book was being compiled. They provided me with mountains of information and showed a great enthusiasm for their particular areas as well. Thanks are also due to East Lothian Tourist Board and Marius Alexander for extra pictures. I also received much appreciated help from Michael Starrett, manager of the Pentland Hills Regional Park, and from Helen Rowbotham, ranger for British Waterways.

HMSO acknowleges the financial assistance of Lothian Regional Council towards the publishing of the book.

All facts have been checked as far as possible but the author and publishers cannot be held responsible for any errors, however caused.

British Library Cataloguing in Publication Data

A catalogue record for this book is available from the British Library

ISBN 0 11 495220 5

CONTENTS

The book's title reflects its coverage. Edinburgh is Scotland's capital city (whatever Glasgow may say about that), but Lothian is a proud historical entity, greater than the sum of its three distinctive parts. Each of these – West, Mid and East – rightly claims an identity, but to me they also weave together into the wider area called Lothian, and they wrap comfortingly around the old city like a green plaid.

Using the book is easy. The walks are of moderate length and most can easily be tackled by families even with quite young children. The information panels give a summary of the type of terrain to be encountered and advice as to whether strong footwear is needed (it is, in a number of cases, especially after wet conditions).

There are no high hills, but if venturing into open country, use common sense and if conditions are really bad, perhaps it might be better to return another day. All the walks benefit from good conditions, not least so that you can enjoy the views to the full. Please keep dogs under close control at all times.

I also show where refreshments can be obtained, and give outline details of public transport. Nearly all the walks are accessible by train or bus and in the case of the linear walks, return is by the same method. The bus/train network in and around Edinburgh is excellent, and I would urge readers to use it whenever possible. The only difficulty likely to be encountered is the peculiar (to me) system found on some buses of not giving change. Opening hours of visitor attractions are listed, with the proviso that these can change from year to year.

While researching and writing this book I have made many discoveries. When I started I was sure it would be interesting, but I was less certain about the quality of the walking. I need not have worried: if you take all these walks you will discover not only Edinburgh and Lothian's past but also its present in the shape of the facilities provided for your enjoyment. May you gain as much in so doing as I have in the writing.

ROGER SMITH

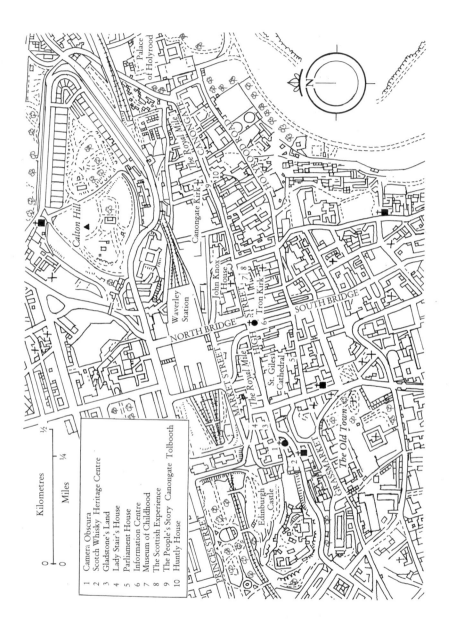

Kilometres

Miles

1 Camera Obscura
2 Scotch Whisky Heritage Centre
3 Gladstone's Land
4 Lady Stair's House
5 Parliament House
6 Information Centre
7 Museum of Childhood
8 The Scottish Experience
9 The People's Story Canongate Tolbooth
10 Huntly House

THE OLD TOWN

I t may seem odd to start a book of walks by not describing the route of the first walk. But an exploration of Edinburgh's Old Town should be very much a personal discovery. Up and down the Royal Mile, there are so many closes, lanes and wynds to dive into that it is far better to leave readers to discover them for themselves.

I suggest you start at the Tron Kirk, at the junction of the High Street and North Bridge. The church was designed by John and Alexander Mylne and was consecrated in 1641, taking its name from the city's public weighbeam, or tron, which stood nearby. Its original wooden steeple was destroyed by fire in 1824.

The church has not been used for worship since 1952 and is now the Old Town Information Centre. Here you can collect masses of useful information, including an excellent free leaflet called the Old Town of Edinburgh which itself suggests walking routes and lists the opening hours of all the attractions. Within the church, excavations have revealed the route of Marlin's Wynd, a narrow street which was covered over when the church was built.

I suggest that when you come out of the Tron Kirk, you turn left and go up to the top of the High Street to visit the castle, then work your way down the north side of the Royal Mile to the entrance to Holyrood, then return up the south side.

As you start the walk, try to cast your mind back two and a half centuries. The Royal Mile had the same shape, running down from the castle to the abbey and palace at its foot. Instead of buses, lorries and cars, horses and carts clogged the street; many people went around on foot.

The entire life of the city of Edinburgh was concentrated here, with people living in high tenements, crammed together with only basic sanitation: a scene sparkling with life yet at the same time squalid by today's standards. Only a little further

INFORMATION

Distance: About 5 km (3 miles).
Start and finish: Tron Kirk (Old Town Information Centre).
Terrain: City streets. No special footwear needed.
Refreshments: Wide selection of pubs, cafes and restaurants en route.

Opening hours: There are too many attractions on the walk to be listed here. Information is available at the Tron Kirk or the Tourism Centre outside Waverley Station. Places you may wish to visit include Edinburgh Castle, the Camera Obscura, Scotch Whisky Heritage Centre, Gladstone's Land, Lady Stair's House, St Giles Cathedral, John Knox House, the Scottish Experience, the Museum of Childhood, the People's Story and Huntly House.
Walking tours: Mercat Tours, (0131) 661 4541. All tours start from the Mercat Cross beside St Giles Cathedral.
Edinburgh Old Town Renewal Trust, 8 Advocates Close, 357 High Street, Edinburgh EH1 1PS, (0131) 225 8818.

The Old Town skyline.

east, Canongate, which you traverse on this walk, was a separate area, outside the main city.

At the top of the street stands Edinburgh Castle, perched at the highest point of a classic 'crag and tail' volcanic formation. The site was fortified at least as early as the Iron Age, and the oldest part of the castle, St Margaret's Chapel, dates back to the 12th century. A tour of the castle takes in the Great Hall, the Honours of Scotland, the National War Memorial, the great gun called Mons Meg, and the room where Mary Queen of Scots gave birth to her son James, who united the crowns of Scotland and England in 1603. Edinburgh's one o'clock gun is still fired from the battlements daily, and every summer the superb Military Tattoo is held at the castle.

Just outside the Castle gate is the Camera Obscura, housed in an 18th century building. It projects a moving image of Edinburgh, and there is also a holography exhibition. Opposite is the Scotch Whisky Heritage Centre, which tells the full story of Scotland's national drink.

A little further down, Castlehill becomes Lawnmarket. Here you can visit Gladstone's Land, a 17th century merchant's house restored by the National Trust for Scotland and furnished in the style of the period. Behind it is Lady Stair's House, now an intriguing writers' museum containing memorabilia of Robert Burns, Sir Walter Scott, Robert Louis Stevenson and other famous authors.

St Giles Cathedral.

The view down the Royal Mile is dominated by St Giles Cathedral; like the castle, it has been a major part of Edinburgh's life for nearly a thousand years. Here John Knox preached his reforming sermons and here the Knights of the Most Ancient and Noble Order of the Thistle still hold their annual service. The knights' stalls, elaborately carved in oak, can be seen, and there is superb stained glass.

Behind the cathedral is Parliament Square, which from 1639 to 1707 was indeed the political centre of the Scottish nation, and still serves an important role as the legal centre of Edinburgh. Parliament House itself and the beautiful Signet Library are sometimes open to view.

Crossing the North Bridge junction – a relatively recent addition, dating from the time of the development of the New Town (see walk 2) – High Street becomes Canongate, its name coming from the canons of Holyrood Abbey. This was until the 19th century very much a separate community. It is now firmly linked to the city centre. The Scandic Crown Hotel is a major recent development carefully designed to blend with the historic street.

As you walk down, you will reach John Knox House, where the Netherbow Port, a gateway into the city, once stood, and the fine old Canongate Kirk. There are intriguing museums including The People's Story, housed in the Canongate Tolbooth, which tells the story of the working folk of Edinburgh; and the Museum of Childhood, the first in the world to devote itself to the child's world.

John Knox House.

There is no space here to fully describe all the many historic houses, shops, museums and alleyways that make up the Old Town. They can only be fully explored and discovered on foot, and several excellent guided walking tours are available, including one devoted to ghosts and ghouls. A couple of hours with a qualified guide is a memorable experience.

But then the Old Town is a memorable place. And happily it is being well cared for under the auspices of the Edinburgh Old Town Renewal Trust, which aims to preserve the best of the past while maintaining the area as a place for people to live and work.

This is a happy development, which would surely please the city fathers of the mid 18th century who had the foresight and vision to expand across the marshes which are now Princes Street Gardens and commission the building of the elegant New Town, the subject of walk 2.

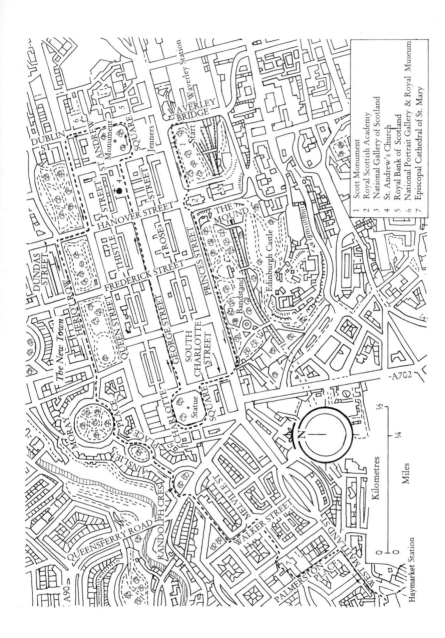

1 Scott Monument
2 Royal Scottish Academy
3 National Gallery of Scotland
4 St. Andrew's Church
5 Royal Bank of Scotland
6 National Portrait Gallery & Royal Museum
7 Episcopal Cathedral of St. Mary

THE NEW TOWN

By the mid 18th century, conditions in the Old Town were becoming intolerable, with squalor and overcrowding everywhere. The tall old houses were unsafe too: in September 1751 a six-storey tenement in the High Street collapsed and others had to be pulled down. It was a time for expansion.

The expansion needed men of vision, and fortunately they were to hand, not least in the person of George Drummond, six times Lord Provost, who pressed for a comprehensive design for a New Town on land acquired by the city to the north. A competition was held, and was won by a young architect, James Craig. His plan for a grid pattern of spacious streets with fine town houses was accepted in 1767, a year after Drummond's death, and building continued for the next 30 years.

The area has survived the wear and tear of two centuries remarkably well and is recognised as one of the finest Georgian townscapes to be found anywhere

INFORMATION

Distance: 4 km (2.5 miles).

Start: Waverley Station.

Finish: Haymarket Station.

Terrain: Roads and surfaced paths. No special footwear needed.

Refreshments: Selection of pubs and cafes along the route. **Note:** Car parking in central Edinburgh is difficult, and it is recommended that public transport is used. There is metered parking in many of the New Town streets, and the walk can be joined at any point.

Opening hours: *Scott Monument:* Mon-Sat Apr-Sep 0900–1800, Oct-Mar 0900–1500. Sun 1200–1700 Jun-Sep only. Admission charge. *Royal Scottish Academy, National Gallery of Scotland, National Portrait Gallery and Royal Museum:* All year, Mon-Sat 1000–1700. Sun 1400–1700. Admission charge to RSA: others free. *Georgian House:* Apr-Oct Mon-Sat 1000–1700, Sun 1400–1700. Admission charge.

The Scott Monument.

in Britain. The street names were originally chosen to symbolise the union: Rose Street is matched by Thistle Street and so on. As you will read however, this plan was not fully followed through. This walk explores the area and in so doing encounters a bewildering panoply of historical characters, each of whom warrants a book in their own right.

From Waverley Station walk up the ramp now used by vehicles for access, cross Waverley Bridge and turn right then left to enter East Princes Street Gardens. The station, covering 10 ha, is the second largest in Britain and was built between 1892 and 1902.

As you enter the gardens, look across Princes Street to see Jenners. The business dates from 1834 and the building itself celebrates its centenary in 1995. Designed by W. H. Beattie, its frontage is based on the Bodleian Library in Oxford. It was a revelation when it opened, with electric light, air conditioning and lifts.

Walk along the short distance to the Scott Monument. Designed by George Meikle Kemp, who later drowned in the Union Canal, the monument and spire rise to 60 m, and in 1844 cost £16,000. Scott's statue in Carrara marble, by Sir John Steell, shows him wrapped in a plaid with his staghound Maida at his feet. The exterior bears 64 characters from Scott's books or from Scottish history. The view from the top is extensive.

Sir Walter Scott

The walk continues past statues of Adam Black, publisher and twice Lord Provost, and of John Wilson, a popular 19th century writer under the pseudonym Christopher North, to cross The Mound and reach the Royal Scottish Academy and the National Gallery, which house superb art collections. Both were designed by W. H. Playfair, the RSA in 1826 and the Gallery in 1859. In front is a large statue of Queen Victoria by Steell, unveiled in 1844.

Enter East Princes Street Gardens. Before the New Town was built, this was the Nor' Loch, a fetid swamp and rubbish tip. The gardens were laid out by James

Skene; in this corner is the world's oldest floral clock, dating from 1903. The motif, using 20,000 plants, changes each year.

Across the gardens, Castle Rock rears up steeply. In the gardens are a memorial to the Royal Scots; the Ross Bandstand, busy with concerts in the summer; and the Scottish-American War Memorial, entitled The Call and paid for by Americans with Scottish roots in 1927.

Continue through the gardens, passing a Scots Greys Boer War memorial and statues to the pioneer educationalist Dr Thomas Guthrie and to Sir James Simpson, the first to use chloroform as an anaesthetic in 1847. It gained general approval when used by Queen Victoria at the birth of Prince Leopold in 1853.

Leave the gardens and cross Princes Street. Many of the streets in the New Town are named for Hanoverian royalty. Princes Street was called St Giles Street by Craig, but the name was changed at the request of George III to honour his two sons. The younger was the Duke of York who 'had ten thousand men', etc. in the well-known nursery rhyme.

Walk up South Charlotte Street to reach Charlotte Square, an elegant 1791 design by Robert Adam, who died the following year without seeing it completed. The north side is especially fine. No. 5 is the headquarters of the National Trust for Scotland; no. 6, Bute House, is the official residence of the Secretary of State for Scotland; and no. 7 has been restored by the Trust as its Georgian House, furnished in the original style of the period.

Charlotte Square.

The square is named for George III's queen, who bore him 15 children. This too was not Craig's name. He chose St George's Square as a counterpart to St Andrew's Square at the far end of George Street. In the centre of the 12-sided garden – used biennially for the Edinburgh Book Fair – is a statue of Prince Albert.

Continue along George Street, designed by Craig to be wide enough for a carriage and four horses to turn. It is also named for George III, who reigned for 60 years (1760–1820) but sadly suffered from insanity in later years. Each of the intersections carries a statue. The first (again by Steell) is to the Rev Thomas Chalmers, a remarkable man who led the Disruption of the Church in 1843 and became a Professor of both Divinity and Mathematics. During his life he raised over £300,000 (the equivalent of £30 million today) to build 220 new churches.

The next statue is on the corner of Frederick Street, named for George III's father. It is to William Pitt, Britain's youngest ever Prime Minister, who took that office aged just 24 in 1784 and held it for 20 years.

George IV

Next is a bronze statue of George IV by Sir Francis Chantrey. George IV was the first monarch since 1650 to visit Scotland when he came to Edinburgh, dressed in a kilt and pink tights, in 1822. He was described as 'a hard drinking, swearing man who preferred a girl and a bottle to politics and a sermon'. No fewer than 25 streets in Edinburgh are named after him, using his many titles. Crossing here is Hanover Street, marking the dynasty that extended from George I's accession in 1714 to the death of William IV in 1837.

Continue past St Andrew's Church, where the 1843 Disruption started, to St Andrew Square. In its centre is a 41 m high monument to Henry Dundas, 1st Viscount Melville, who as Lord President virtually ruled Scotland from 1782 to 1805. The monument, by William Burn, was based on Trajan's Column in Rome and was paid for, in 1821, by officers and men of the Royal Navy. How willing they were is not recorded.

The Royal Bank building in St Andrew Square.

Across the square, which lacks the symmetry of Charlotte Square, is the headquarters of the Royal Bank of Scotland. The house was built in 1774 for Sir Lawrence Dundas. Shortly after moving in he actually lost the house in a card game with General John Scott but the general allowed him to keep it on condition that Dundas built Scott a new house, which he did, in Dublin Street. An expensive gamble. Just off the

square in Thistle Court are the first buildings erected in
the New Town, in 1767.

Walk down North St Andrew Street to Queen Street.
On the right are the National Portrait Gallery. and the
Royal Museum of Scotland. Turn left into Queen
Street (named for Queen Charlotte again) and turn
right into Queen Street Gardens East, and left into
Heriot Row. For once we leave the Hanoverians. Built
between 1803 and 1808, the handsome Row is named
for George Heriot, a wealthy 16th century jeweller
known as 'Jinglin' Geordie', who founded the school
named after him.

Continue to Moray Place, an elegant 12-sided square
designed by James Gillespie Graham and named for the
Earl of Moray, half-brother of Mary, Queen of Scots.
Continue round the square and across Ainslie Place to
Randolph Crescent, named for another Earl of Moray,
nephew and henchman of Robert the Bruce.

Go left round the crescent and cross Queensferry Road
into Melville Street. This area is known as the Western
New Town and was laid out by Robert Brown for
William Walker in the early 19th century. The street is
named for Henry Dundas but the statue halfway along
it is of his son Robert and is, like so many others in
Edinburgh, by Steell.

To each side, Walker Street marks the man who owned
the land. At the end of Melville Street is the very large
Episcopal Cathedral of St Mary, designed by Sir George
Gilbert Scott in the Early Pointed style. It cost over
£100,000 and was largely built between 1874–79. Later
additions include a Chapel of Resurrection by Sir
Robert Lorimer. The cathedral has a superb peal of
bells.

The cathedral fronts on to Palmerston Place, named for
Lord Palmerston, three times Prime Minister during
Victoria's reign (she is said to have disliked him
intensely). Walk down to West Maitland Street and
turn right for Haymarket Station and the end of the
walk.

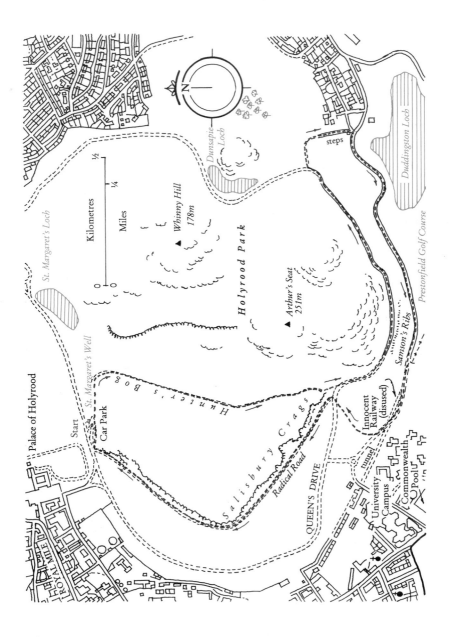

HOLYROOD PARK

Although this walk does not actually take in Holyrood Palace, the Queen's official residence when she is in Edinburgh, the palace and abbey are so close by that to combine them with the walk makes a logical outing. The walk concentrates on the lovely open space of Holyrood Park. It tours the park but does not go up to the summit of Arthur's Seat, which is visited on walk 4.

From the car park, cross the road and head slightly left to see St Margaret's Well, a unique well house dating from the 15th century. It was originally at Restalrig and its design is a miniature copy of St Triduana's aisle there. The well was moved to Holyrood Park in 1860.

Climb up behind the well to a surfaced path. Turn left and follow the path as it curves rightwards into the valley known as Hunter's Bog. Arthur's Seat looms impressively above and to the left. Walk up the valley – long used as a rifle range – towards its head, and when the path begins to curve back leftward, go half right on a good grass path that climbs to the obvious col ahead.

At the col, go ahead on another grass path. After 80 m you are presented with a wonderful view of the Castle and much of Edinburgh, with Salisbury Crags (your return route) framing the picture to the right. Join the road ahead – the Queen's Drive – and continue along it as it curves left, giving excellent views southwards to the Pentland Hills.

Below and to the right is Prestonfield Golf Course and beyond it part of the campus of Edinburgh University and the Commonwealth Pool, built for the 1970 Commonwealth Games and now a much-used recreational facility. Shattered crags rear up to the left. Before long, Duddingston Loch and its marshes are seen below and then the view eastwards along the Firth of Forth opens out.

INFORMATION

Distance: 5 km (3 miles).

Start and finish: Main car park at Holyrood entrance to the park.

Terrain: Good paths. Special footwear not necessary.

Public transport: Buses from the city centre (LRT 1 and 6, McLeans 60) pass the park entrance.

Refreshments: None en route. Nearest in Royal Mile.

Opening hours: *Holyrood Palace:* Mon-Sat 0930–1715, Sun 1030–1630. The palace may be closed in the second half of both May and June, and at other times when the Queen is in residence or official functions are taking place.

Edinburgh from the park.

Pied Wagtail

When the railing on the right ends, go right down a path to the boundary wall. Turn right and walk down the very long flight of steps. Perhaps you will count them as you go. I always end up with a different number, but I think there are about 200!

On reaching the road at the bottom, at the Duddingston entrance to the park, turn right. You might like to cross the road and go down to the loch, but it is best to return to the road – the lochside path, such as it is, is intermittent and often very muddy.

Duddingston Loch is a nature reserve managed by the Scottish Wildlife Trust in association with the city. It attracts very large flocks of birds in winter, species seen here including pochard and greylag geese. The reedy areas – once part of the loch – draw smaller birds such as the pied wagtail.

The road runs along the side of the loch, with the rock feature known as Samson's Ribs rising very steeply to the right. These basalt columns, similar to those seen in Fingal's Cave on the island of Staffa though perhaps not quite as perfect, are formed when molten rock left in a volcanic vent after an eruption slowly cools.

Further along the road to the left you can see a tunnel entrance. This was the line of the charmingly-named Innocent Railway. A short diversion enables you to look into the tunnel, now a path and cycleway. The railway ran from Edinburgh to Dalkeith and got its name because the carriages were originally horse-drawn – the 'innocent' means of transport – in an age which still thought steam engines highly dangerous.

The railway opened in 1831, and this was the earliest tunnel of its kind in Scotland. It is 518 m long. Like many other small lines, the railway closed in the 1960s.

From the tunnel, take the path by the fence. At the large expanse of mown grass, leave the road and head right, up towards the crags. Keep to the right edge of this mown area, curving right to cross another road and head up to the start of the path rising below the crags.

This path, known as the Radical Road, provides a most exciting finale to the walk as it makes an airy traverse below the crags, giving excellent views out over the city and the unmistakeable skyline of the Old Town. The path was the idea of Sir Walter Scott. Concerned with the growing radicalism of unemployed men following the Napoleonic Wars, he thought that useful work such as this would turn their minds away from dissent as well as providing them with much-needed income.

In geological terms, Salisbury Crags are a dolerite sill formed of hard rock left behind when the softer lava screes eroded away. During the 19th century there was extensive quarrying here, much of the stone going to pave the streets of London and other English cities. This quarrying left the rock faces even sharper, and also provided a natural arena for rock climbers.

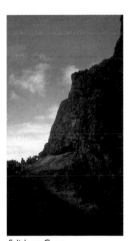

Salisbury Crags.

The crags were indeed important as a training ground in the early years of Scottish mountaineering a century ago, and many pioneers of the sport practised their skills here before heading off to higher mountains both in Scotland and abroad. In recent years climbing has been banned to avoid risk to both climbers and others using the area, but from August 1994 climbing was allowed again for a trial period of a year, in the South Quarry only, so you may see the 'rock gymnasts' inching up the vertical faces.

Another observer of the rock faces was James Hutton, the pioneering geologist (1726–1797). His researches here led him to present a paper to the Royal Society of Edinburgh in 1785 suggesting the igneous nature of the rock – commonly accepted now, but a revolutionary idea at the time.

You can perhaps think of Hutton, Scott and other famous names as you take the steady climb over the top of the rise and then down, steadily at first and then more steeply, enjoying the views all the while, to return to the car park below at the end of this tour of Holyrood Park, a priceless asset at the city's heart.

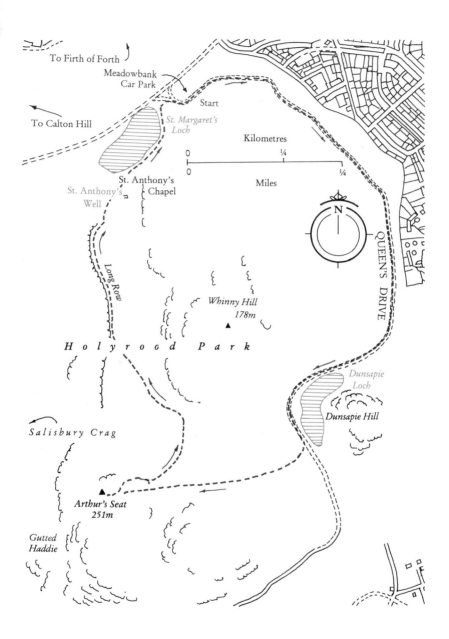

To Firth of Forth

Meadowbank
Car Park

To Calton Hill

Start

St. Margaret's
Loch

Kilometres

0   ¼

0   ¼

Miles

St. Anthony's
Chapel

St. Anthony's
Well

N

QUEEN'S DRIVE

Long Row

Whinny Hill
178m

H o l y r o o d   P a r k

Dunsapie
Loch

Dunsapie Hill

Salisbury Crag

Arthur's Seat
251m

Gutted
Haddie

ARTHUR'S SEAT

Despite its modest height, Arthur's Seat is a summit eagerly sought by thousands of visitors to Edinburgh and also regularly climbed by residents of the city, for the exercise it provides and for the superb views it commands. The hill, with its notable landscape companion, Salisbury Crags (walk 3), is the dominant feature of Edinburgh when seen from any distance, and forms part of the skyline on many of the walks in this book.

The walk starts from the free car park at the Meadowbank end of the park. From the east end of the car park (nearest the houses) climb the steps up to the road and turn left. The road, which is narrow and not infrequently closed to traffic, especially in winter, climbs steadily round several bends. You are unlikely to have it to yourself, for the park is heavily used by walkers, joggers, cyclists and dogs of all shapes and sizes.

As you climb, a fine view opens up to your left along the shore of the Firth of Forth to Portobello and beyond, with Berwick Law a very clear cone. At the top of the slope, the road bends right with Arthur's Seat now clear ahead – usually with two files of people, one going up and the other coming down!

On the left, hidden by the large craggy knoll of Dunsapie Hill at first, is Dunsapie Loch, always busy with birds. It holds large numbers of swans, geese and ducks and in winter the population is further boosted by migrating greylag geese. Many of the birds will come fearlessly towards you looking for food.

INFORMATION

Distance: 5 km (3 miles).

Start and finish: Meadowbank car park, Holyrood Park.

Terrain: Paths of various kinds. Strong footwear advised, especially in wet conditions. Steep ascent to the summit of Arthur's Seat.

Public transport: Any bus from the city centre going along London Road will pass the Meadowbank entrance to the park. Services include LRT 4, 5, 15, 26, 43, 44, 45, 51, 63, 66. SMT 44, 66, 129. LOW/SMT 124, 125.

Refreshments: None en route. Nearest in Meadowbank.

Looking across the city from Arthur's Seat.

Top: Dunsapie Loch.

Above: Looking east
from the summit.

From the loch, take any one of several paths leading up to Arthur's Seat. They are all steep, but there is no need to hurry, and compensation lies in the ever-expanding views over the city and the Firth to Fife and beyond.

At the top, which is crowned by an Ordnance Survey triangulation pillar and a view indicator, you are standing on the central vent of an ancient volcano formed here about 350 million years ago – so the geologists tell us. Such timespans are beyond the comprehension of most folk, but Edinburgh has been extensively studied by geologists and its formation and early landscape history are well documented.

The volcano would originally have been much higher, of course. The twin summits called the Lion's Head and the Lion's Haunch are the remnants of its vents. Calton Hill nearby is, it seems, a displaced fragment of the same volcano. Over millennia, the volcanic cone built up through successive eruptions to a height well above the surrounding plains, and formed the hill we know today. Erosion and alteration still goes on: as recently as 1744 a torrential cloudburst scoured out the gully below the summit now known as the Gutted Haddie.

The view from the summit takes in most of the city, with the 'crag and tail' formation of Castle Rock and the Royal Mile clear, and sweeps round to the Firth and its islands, the Fife hills beyond, the two great bridges, Bass Rock and Berwick Law and on to the Pentland Hills to the south. The other ancient stumps forming the Seven Hills of Edinburgh can be seen; Blackford and Braid, Craiglockhart and Corstorphine. It is a view to be savoured at all times of the year, in the sparkling air of spring, the haze of summer which may hide the more distant features, the cool of autumn or the sharpness of winter, perhaps with a dusting of snow on the Pentland tops.

When you are ready to leave, retrace your steps partway down the hill, but keeping more to the left, looking for the path down into the small valley to your left. This valley is your return route and is gained by curving left from the summit path and then turning left at a path junction at a clear col.

As you descend, Arthur's Seat rears up impressively behind you. The name may well come from the legend of King Arthur and his Knights, heroes of ancient Britain, who are said to be sleeping here (and in at least a dozen other places of the same name), waiting for the call to arms to defend the land again. Their sleep must be profound, for there have been plenty of opportunities for them over the past thousand years or so.

Follow the path down the valley. On your left are the small crags known as the Long Row, sedimentary rocks which have remained while other softer rocks have eroded away. Near the foot of the valley divert right and climb to see the ruin of St Anthony's Chapel. Before you do so, look at the layered rocks below it, which demonstrate clearly the sequence of lava and ash laid down all those millions of years ago.

The chapel, on a mound above St Margaret's Loch, is an ancient foundation probably dating from the 16th century, said to have been founded by the Hospitallers of St Anthony, based at Leith. From here they could see ships coming in to the Leith Docks. It has been the scene of several weddings or blessing ceremonies in recent years; below it on the hill is a spring called St Anthony's Well. From the chapel there is a particularly fine view of Calton Hill and the skyline of the Old Town, leading your eye up the slope of the Royal Mile to the Castle on its volcanic rock.

From the chapel, you can either return to the valley and walk round the loch by the road, or go down more steeply to the right to reach the loch. Like Dunsapie, there are many waterfowl here, all of them eager to take whatever titbits may be offered. Giving them something is a pleasant way to round off the walk.

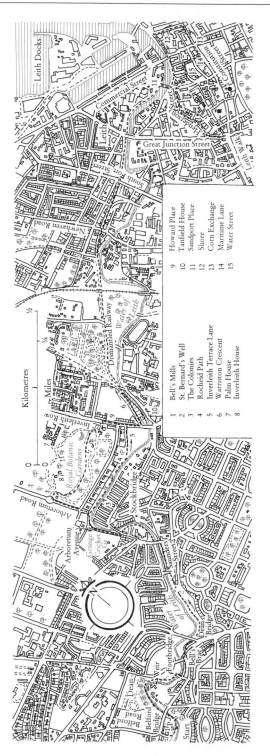

Leith Docks

Commercial Street

Leith

Hospital

Great Junction Street

South Fort Street

Newhaven Road

Leith Walk

Commercial Street

Coburg Street

Water of Leith

Dismantled Railway

Miles

Kilometres

Inverleith Row

Royal Botanic Gardens

Arboretum Road

Arboretum Avenue

Grange Cricket Gr

Stockbridge

Saunders Street

Water of Leith

Dean Bridge

Bell's Brae

Footbridge

Weir

Dean

Belford Road

Belford Bridge

Start

1	Bell's Mills	
2	St. Bernard's Well	
3	The Colonies	
4	Rocheid Path	
5	Inverleith Terrace Lane	
6	Warriston Crescent	
7	Palm House	
8	Inverleith House	

9	Howard Place	
10	Tanfield House	
11	Sandport Place	
12	Shore	
13	Corn Exchange	
14	Maritime Lane	
15	Water Street	

THE WATER OF LEITH I: DEAN TO LEITH

The Water of Leith Walkway is a splendid recreational asset for Edinburgh. Managed by the District Council with support from other agencies and from the Water of Leith Conservation Trust, the full route extends for 18 km from Balerno to the docks at Leith. This walk covers the last part of the walkway: walk 10 takes in another section, from Balerno to Slateford.

To start the walk, go down Bell's Mills at the side of the Edinburgh Hilton Hotel and across the car park to the sign on the riverside path – left to Dean Village and Stockbridge, right to the Museum of Modern Art. Turn left and walk past the back of the hotel, by a weir and under the Belford Bridge. Rebuilt in 1855–57, it carries the city and royal crests on both sides.

A footbridge leads to the houses of Dean Village. Do not cross it but go straight on. The path is a quiet world in a noisy city, with many trees. The main sound is often birdsong. The river curves sharply right and then tumbles over another weir with a lade on the left as the path descends. This area was built upon milling, and there were once as many as 11 flour mills in Dean.

Pass under a footbridge, then go up to the left and cross the bridge, which is 18th century. Turn left along the riverbank and reach a cobbled road (Hawthornbank Brae). At Bell's Brae, follow the sign to St Bernard's Well and Stockbridge, noting the inscription on the lintel of the house to the right. This was Baxters' Tolbooth, the former headquarters of the baking industry, and the inscription reads 'God bless the Baxters of Edinburgh who built this Hous 1675'. There were formerly mills in this area, and Stewart's Coach House here, a handsome 1881 building, has been beautifully restored as offices.

INFORMATION

Distance: 5.5 km (3.5 miles).

Start: Belford Bridge (if arriving by car, park nearby).

Finish: Leith Docks.

Terrain: Streets and good paths. No special footwear needed.

Public transport: Buses LRT 13 (not Sundays) go from the city centre to Belford Road, or there are numerous services to Dean Bridge on the Queensferry Road. Numerous services from Leith back to St Andrew Square.

Refreshments: Selection of pubs and cafes in both Dean and Leith. Seasonal snack bar in the Royal Botanic Gardens.

The Water of Leith at Belford Bridge.

Go down Miller Row and pass under Telford's superb Dean Bridge, built in 1832 and commissioned by Sir John Learmonth, Lord Provost of Edinburgh, who owned the land to the west; wishing to develop it, he needed a better link with the city centre. He got a classic design from the master engineer, 136 m long and, at over 30 m, one of the highest in the world at the time. Unfortunately for Learmonth, his expected building boom did not take place. The bridge is hollow and today's city engineers regularly inspect it from the inside. You can see from the top of the arches how the bridge was strengthened for modern traffic.

Continue along the path and in 400 m reach St Bernard's Well, a mineral spring over which Alexander Nasmyth constructed a Doric rotunda, commissioned by the famous judge Lord Gardenstone, in 1789. After falling into disrepair, the rotunda was restored in 1888, and at that time D.W.Stevenson's statue of Hygeia, the Greek goddess of good health, was added. The restoration was paid for by a prominent local citizen, William Nelson, and an inscription nearby records his generosity in gifting the well and surrounds 'to the Corporation for the benefit of the citizens of Edinburgh for all time coming'.

Continue on the path right beside the river for 200 m, go under a bridge and along Saunders Street to reach Stockbridge, a part of Edinburgh which retains a village atmosphere. Cross the road at the traffic lights, turn left over the bridge and immediately, beside the TSB building with the charming tower, go down steps to regain the riverside path. The artist Sir Henry Raeburn lived in Stockbridge and knew this area well.

Go up to the road at Falshaw Bridge (1877, reconstructed 1956), turn left and then right into Arboretum Avenue, with Grange Cricket Ground behind the wall to the left. The street name gives a hint of what lies ahead. Across the river you see one of a whole series of little terraces known as the Colonies. They were built between 1861 and 1911 by the Edinburgh Co-Operative Building Company as a social experiment to provide better housing for working-class people.

Swing right and left with the road. If you wish to continue beside the river, go right through a gate and follow the tree-lined Rocheid Path, with the terraces of the Colonies across the river. The path is named for James Rocheid, who built Inverleith House (see below) and also owned the Craigleith Quarries. After 600 m, the path leaves the river and swings left and right along Inverleith Terrace Lane to reach Inverleith Row. Cross the road, turn right and first left into Warriston Crescent.

However, I suggest an alternative which adds interest to the walk. Continue up Arboretum Avenue, cross the road at the junction and walk up Arboretum Road to the west gate of the Royal Botanic Gardens. Enter the gardens (admission is free) and turn right. There are toilets here. Take the left fork and follow this broad path as it curves through the gardens. There are many fine specimen trees and you will often see squirrels here. These animals have become so accustomed to people that the bolder ones will take a titbit from your hand.

Partway along, a new area for the garden's collection of Chinese plants is being developed, sponsored by Dawson International plc. Past this area, take the right fork and then go straight on to the east gate; or, of course, you can explore the gardens, the arboretum and exhibitions at your leisure.

There is much to see. The buildings range from the typically Victorian iron and glass Palm House (1858, Robert Matheson) to the large new glasshouses, designed by George Pearce and opened in 1965. Inverleith House, the mansion in the gardens, dates from 1774 and was designed by David Henderson. From 1960 to 1984 it housed the National Gallery of Modern Art, now sited off Belford Road.

At the east gate is a seat in memory of Mrs Isa Caldwell, who died in 1991 at the great age of 105.

A riot of colour in the Botanic Gardens.

Walk out to Inverleith Row, cross it and turn right. This section is called Howard Place: Robert Louis Stevenson was born at no. 8 in November 1850. Turn left into Warriston Crescent, rejoining the riverside route.

Across to the right is Tanfield House, the administrative and data centre of the Standard Life Assurance Company. This award-winning building by the Michael Laird Partnership was officially opened by the Queen on 1 July 1991. Among its innovative features are 'solar blinds' which give automatic protection to staff working at computer screens. The building is on the site of Tanfield Hall, where the first assembly of the Free Church of Scotland was held on 18 May 1843, following the great schism within the established church. The large sculpture outside the building, called Axis Mundi, is by Gerald Ogilvie Laing and represents the apotheosis of the five wise virgins.

Warriston Crescent is a dead-end for cars but not for walkers. On the wall of no. 10 is a plaque marking the stay here in 1848 of the great composer and pianist Chopin. At the road-end follow the sign 'public footpath to Leith', which takes you up to join the trackbed of the former Caledonian Railway. Turn left, fork right and walk along this pleasant path fringed with birch trees.

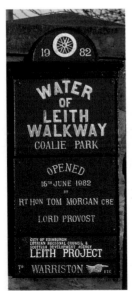

The railway path is followed for nearly two kilometres, keeping straight on at cross-paths. After 800 m, the river curves in again from the right, but only briefly. Pass under Newhaven Road and then in a further 400 m, under South Fort Street, where the bridge shows a remarkable triple development.

In a further 200 m, the river, now very much broader than when you last saw it, is rejoined for the final stage of the walk. Cross at Sandport Place and turn left down the opposite bank. On the far side of the river at Commercial Street is the handsome Doric-style customs house (Robert Reid, 1810–12).

Leith has been Edinburgh's port for centuries, and was not amalgamated into the city until 1920. In 1645, over 2300 people in Leith – nearly half the population – died in the Great Plague. After a period when Leith became somewhat rundown as the dock trade declined, there has been much excellent recent development and restoration. As a finale, a brief tour of part of the area rounds off the walk nicely. Continue down the Shore past the Edinburgh, a floating restaurant. On the right is the Signal Tower, built as a windmill by Robert Mylne in 1686 and fortified during the Napoleonic Wars.

Leith.

Turn right into Tower Street, and right again into Constitution Street to reach a junction with a statue of Robert Burns. On the left is the imposing former Corn Exchange (Peddie and Kinnear, 1860). Continue up Constitution Street and turn right into Maritime Lane. Go left into Water Street and at the corner of Burgess Street find Lamb's House. Built by a merchant, Andro Lamb, in the early 17th century, it was given to the National Trust for Scotland in 1958. The Trust had the building restored by Robert Hurd and partners and it it is now in regular use as an old people's day centre.

At the end of Burgess Street, you are back at the Shore. Turn left, continue along Henderson Street, and go left with it to reach Great Junction Street. Go left through the Newkirkgate Shopping Centre to see, on the right, South Leith Parish Church, a large and impressive building which dates back as far as 1483. The older parts are largely hidden by Thomas Hamilton's 1848 remodelling, which included a square-topped tower. He is said to have modelled the roof on St Isaac's Cathedral in St Petersburg, Russia. The church is undergoing extensive restoration, with assistance from Historic Scotland.

Return through the shopping centre to the main road, from where many bus services run up the broad Leith Walk back to the city centre.

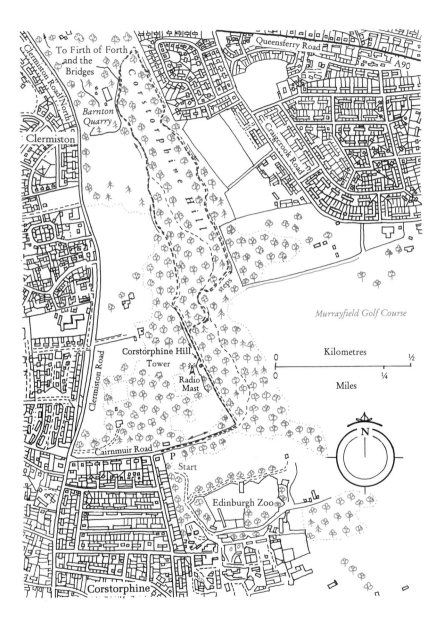

CORSTORPHINE HILL

Corstorphine Hill, a low wooded ridge, is a notable Edinburgh landmark. It is managed as a public open space by the District Council, and this walk could easily be combined with a visit to Edinburgh's famous and extensive zoo, which sits at the south-eastern corner of the hill.

The walk starts at the small parking area at the end of Cairnmuir Road, off Clermiston Road. Go through the gate and follow the path between the dyke on the left and the high fence on the right (the Zoo boundary).

At a fork in 200 m, go left to enter a large open area. Keep left at two more forks to reach a clear path, and turn left. One of the hill's main characteristics now becomes clear. It possesses a multiplicity of paths, constantly dividing and coming together, which makes precise direction-giving very difficult.

You are aiming for the large radio mast seen ahead. The path you are (probably) on runs under trees: trending right here will lead you to the perimeter fence of the mast, but you may also arrive there by a quite different route!

INFORMATION

Distance: 5 km (3 miles).

Start and finish: Cairnmuir Road, off Clermiston Road.

Terrain: Good paths and tracks. Strong footwear may be needed in wet conditions.

Public transport: Buses LRT 26, 69, 86 and SMT 86 from the city centre to Clermiston Road (service 26A only on Sundays).

Refreshments: None en route. Pubs and cafes in Corstorphine.

Opening Hours: *Corstorphine Hill Tower:* Open 1400–1600 on the last Sunday afternoon of the month, May to September.

Looking west from near the summit of Corstorphine Hill.

Corstorphine Hill Tower.

In any event, go round the right-hand side of the fence to reach Corstorphine Hill Tower, which is heavily screened by trees. The tower, a typically imposing Victorian monument, was erected in 1871 by William Macfie of Clermiston to mark the centenary of Sir Walter Scott's birth, and presented to the city in 1932 – the centenary of Scott's death – by W.G.Walker. Inside the tower, steps lead to a viewing platform at the top. It is occasionally open (see information panel) and from the top you can see much of the city and surrounding area – including, of course, the rather more famous monument to the author on Princes Street.

From the tower, you need to head north along the ridge. There is a fairly clear path for much of the way, but as with other paths on the hill, it wanders about a bit as if unsure of its destiny and occasionally disappears altogether. After leaving the tower, the path drops steeply, then climbs briefly again. The key direction is to keep high on the ridge and not drop off to the sides.

Further along, the path becomes clearer, passing a large grassed area to the left. This gives a good view across the west of the city, and a little further on there are other fine views taking in the two bridges and the Firth.

Go over a clear cross track, ahead on a narrower path, then in 100 m go right through a rocky gully to meet a very clear broad path with wooden edging. Turn left, and rapidly fork right to walk beside a fence round the extensive Barnton Quarry. Whichever way you make your path along the hill, you need to reach this quarry boundary fence and walk rightwards around it.

The constant noise of traffic on Queensferry Road is growing louder. At a junction, with the traffic noise now sounding very close, go sharply right on a broad track which runs along the eastern flank of the hill, below the main slope. This track gives easy, fast walking. There are houses to the left visible through the trees.

Before long the houses are left behind as the track winds around the hill. Go straight over at a junction. The track climbs, joins a fence (on the left) and levels out. It then climbs again to reach a long flight of steps. At the top, go left on another path.

Before long, a break in the trees gives an extensive view of the city across Murrayfield Golf Course on the left. It was at or near this point that Alan Breck parted from David Balfour in Stevenson's famous novel *Kidnapped*, following their many adventures. Leave the main track here and take the path going steeply up to the right. Once back on the ridge, go left for a short distance to the tower, and from there retrace your steps back to the start of the walk.

This is in some senses a frustrating walk, for two main reasons. Firstly, the tree cover on the hill largely masks the views. Secondly, the paths seem to have a mind of their own! But there are compensations. The trees also mask the traffic, and as you wander along the hill you may well see squirrels and a variety of birdlife. There are also many interesting small rock features. And if there is sometimes a feeling of being ever so slightly lost, that only adds to the fun of the walk.

Deep in the Corstorphine Woods.

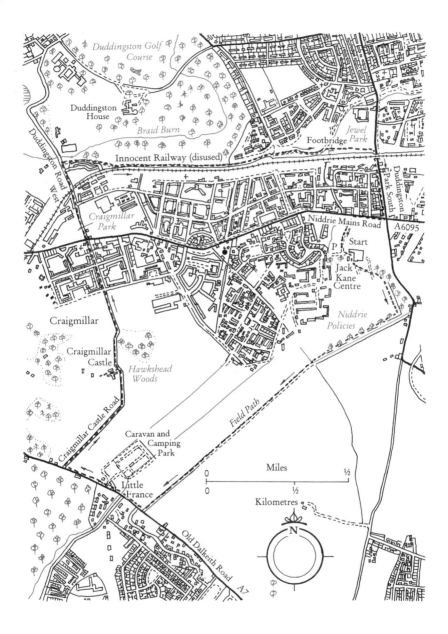

CRAIGMILLAR

This is yet another example of an Edinburgh walk which is surprisingly rural in character, although it does have some urban sections. Its highlight is the splendid Craigmillar Castle, less well known than its counterpart of Edinburgh, but every bit as interesting historically.

The walk starts at the Jack Kane Centre, which acts as a focus for the community in the Niddrie/Craigmillar area and stages many social and arts events. From the centre walk across the open space, heading half left to pick up a path which runs a few metres inside the boundary wall.

Follow this path for about 300 m and then turn right by another wall. If you prefer, for the next section you can walk along the edge of the playing fields rather than in the trees. This large area is known as the Niddrie Policies and is a very valuable public open space.

At the end of the open area, go left on a path and then right to walk across the fields. This field path is an amazing survival: it runs for a full kilometre in a dead straight line, heading south-west. You can see Craigmillar Castle on the hill to the right.

Follow the path all the way to Old Dalkeith Road (the A7), and turn right. The incessant traffic comes as a rude shock after the peaceful field walk. Cross a small burn and pass the Little France Caravan and Camping Park, much used by foreign visitors to Edinburgh. Just past here is a petrol station which has a good shop selling sweets, drinks and ice-cream if you feel in need of some refreshment. In 1566, when Mary, Queen of Scots stayed at the castle, many of her retinue had come from France with her, and so many French accents were heard that the area got its nickname 'Little France'.

Take the next turning right (Craigmillar Castle Road) and walk up towards the castle. Unfortunately the

INFORMATION

Distance: 7 km (4 miles).

Start and finish: Jack Kane Centre, Niddrie Mains Road (large car park).

Terrain: Roads and paths. No special footwear needed.

Public transport: Any bus from the city centre to Niddrie Mains Road. Services include LRT 2, 12, 14, 21, 32 and 52. SMT C3, 131.

Refreshments: Cafe at Jack Kane Centre.

Opening hours: *Craigmillar Castle:* April–Sep Mon–Sat 0930–1830, Sun 1400–1830. Oct–Mar Mon–Sat 0930–1630, Sun 1400–1630. Admission charge.

The field path.

road has no footpath, so walk on the right facing the traffic and proceed with care. The road climbs steadily and bends left before the castle entrance is reached.

Gateway at Craigmillar Castle.

My Edinburgh map states baldly 'Craigmillar Castle (ruin)' but what you see is very much more impressive than that. It's a super castle for children, with lots of wee dark rooms, stairs and turrets to explore. The name comes from Gaelic words meaning 'the high bare rock' and is very appropriate. The view from the roof, taking in almost the whole city, is sensational.

The oldest part of the castle, an L-plan tower, was built by Sir Simon Preston in 1374. Its walls are 3 m thick and its great hall, on the first floor, measures 12 m by 7 m, with a suitably grand fireplace. The door bears the Preston arms of three unicorn heads.

Fifty years later further towers and curtain walls were added, with cannon loops, providing a powerful stronghold. Not strong enough, however, to resist the advances of Hertford during the 'Rough Wooing' in 1544, when much damage was done. The castle was gradually restored, and in 1660 passed to the Gilmour family, who held it until 1946, when it was given to the nation.

The guide on sale at the castle details its history well: one of the major events was in November 1566 when, as mentioned above, Mary, Queen of Scots came here in retreat from Holyrood. She was still shocked at the brutal murder of her courtier Rizzio before her eyes nine months previously, and was ill following the birth of her son, the future James VI, in June. Her supporters, including Bothwell, Huntly and Argyll, met here to plot the murder of Mary's husband, Lord Darnley. The plot became known as the Craigmillar Bond. It is unlikely that the queen was directly involved. Darnley was duly killed in February 1567, and later that year Mary abdicated in favour of the infant James.

When you have explored the castle fully, return to the road and turn left. On the road are Hawkshead

Woods. Until you reach the houses, the road retains a rural air and has more the character of a country lane. The view across Edinburgh is maintained.

Reach the houses of Craigmillar and walk ahead to Niddrie Mains Road. Cross at the traffic lights and continue on Duddingston Road

Arthur's Seat from the Castle.

West, with a small park opposite. Cross the railway by a bridge and in a further 150 m, turn right at the footpath/cycleway sign for Bingham and Musselburgh.

This is a continuation of the Innocent Railway path encountered in walk 3. The path is surfaced and gives good walking, with Duddingston Golf Course visible through the trees to the left. This may be the only golf course originally laid out by Capability Brown. It occupies the parkland surrounding Duddingston House, designed by William Chambers and built in 1763–68 for the Earl of Abercorn. It is interesting to note that King Edward VII seriously considered buying the house, but eventually chose Sandringham in Norfolk instead. It is now a hotel.

In 200 m the 'live' railway is joined and you may see Sprinter trains rattling past on your right, on their way round the Edinburgh suburban circuit. After about a kilometre of very pleasant walking, with trees to both sides for much of the way, the houses of Bingham are seen to the left. Go over a crosspath and continue (signposted to Jewel).

In a further 400 m you reach Jewel Park, another good open space much used for dog walking. It has playing fields as well. Curve left with the path and cross a small burn by a neat latticed footbridge. Walk ahead towards the road, heading rightward to pick up another path. Turn right at the road (Duddingston Park South) and pass under the railway.

In about 300 m, at the next junction, you will see the Jack Kane Centre on the right.

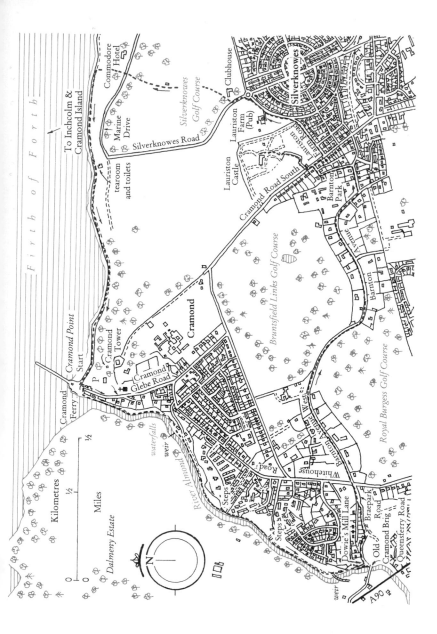

CRAMOND AND SILVERKNOWES

From the car park (alongside which a fort, believed to be Roman, is being excavated) walk out to the road, turn right, cross the road and go down steps to the shore, at the point where the Cramond Ferry makes its short journey across the River Almond. Turn left, pass the Cramond Boat Club and start the walk up the Almond. Looking back, the scene is often busy with boats, and makes a bright and colourful picture. It is hard to believe that this was once an industrial village based on ironworking. All trace of industry has long gone.

The tarmac path winds along beside the river, the peace interrupted by jets overhead making their final approach to Edinburgh Airport. Go through gates into housing, turn right to walk through a neat riverside garden, then continue by the river. You pass several attractive small waterfalls before reaching a weir over which the water drops impressively.

Above the weir the river is broad and still. Waterfowl are often seen here, and you may perhaps see a heron fishing. Soon you are faced with a long, steep flight of steps which surmount a cliff. The path runs along the top of the cliff, looking down on the river below, for about 400 m before an equally long flight of steps takes you back to water level, and a stretch of delightful walking by the sparkling river.

INFORMATION

Distance: 6 km (3.5 miles).

Start and finish: Public car park, Cramond (off Cramond Glebe Road).

Terrain: Pavement and good paths. No special footwear needed.

Public transport: Buses LRT 40 or 41 (41A on Sundays) from George St or Charlotte Sq to head of Cramond Glebe Road, then 500 m walk down to car park.

Refreshments: Pub and cafes in Cramond. Pub at Lauriston Farm. Cafe at Silverknowes.

Opening hours: *Lauriston Castle:* 1 Apr–30 Oct 1100–1700 daily except Friday. 1 Nov–31 Mar 1400–1600 Sat/Sun only. For information on guided tours, Tel: 0131 336 2060.

A weir on the River Almond.

The Cramond Ferry.

The road is reached at Dowie's Mill Lane at another weir, with the Old Cramond Brig ahead. There has been a bridge here for at least 600 years. The one you see today dates from 1619, and has three pointed arches with cutwaters. A couple of hundred metres beyond it and far above, traffic on the Queensferry Road roars past, unaware of the peaceful scene down here. Turn left into Braepark Road, with a children's play area to the right. A small burn runs down on the left between road and houses. The last house is an interesting split-level design with the living space above a large garage.

At the busy Whitehouse Road, cross with care and continue along Barnton Avenue West. One of the houses is called Ben Wyvis and you can only guess at the link between that fine mountain in distant Wester Ross and a leafy Edinburgh suburb.

At the road end, go straight ahead on a broad footpath between two of Edinburgh's golf courses – the Royal Burgess on the right and Bruntsfield Links on the left. The path is enclosed between fences and hedges so you should be safe from wayward shots!

Go through a barrier and continue into Barnton Avenue, which boasts many fine detached houses. The road swings right and then left. Take the next turning left (Barnton Park), cross Cramond Road South (again, with care) and enter the grounds of Lauriston Castle.

Lauriston is a fortified tower house built for Sir Archibald Napier in around 1590. In the 1820s it was transformed by William Burn, who added a large two-storey extension in Jacobean style. In 1902 the castle was purchased by Mr and Mrs W. Reid, and completely renovated. It contains an extensive collection of period furniture, Derbyshire Blue John ornaments and many other interesting things. The Reids left the castle to the nation in 1926, and it is now owned by the City of Edinburgh District Council.

The extensive grounds of the castle, where croquet is sometimes played, include an attractive pond with a statue of a nymph. Opposite the car park is a memorial stone to 14 men of the Bren Gun Carrier Platoon, 1st Battalion, Royal Scots Guards who died in the Burma Campaign in 1943–44.

After looking round the castle and grounds, return to the main entrance, turn left and in 100 m go left again into Lauriston Farm Road. Follow it past Lauriston Farm (now a public house where families are made very welcome and meals are served all day). At the roundabout cross Silverknowes Road, walk round the golf clubhouse and continue across the golf course on a path following short white marker posts. There is a fine view across the Firth of Forth.

Lauriston.

Cross Marine Drive, with the Commodore Hotel on the right, and continue across grass to the broad promenade by the shore. Turn left for the last leg of the walk. Inchcolm is on the right, out in the Firth, and Cramond Island is directly ahead. The two great bridges peep over the trees of Dalmeny Estate.

A sandy spit on the right provides a wonderful play area for dogs and children of all ages; on the left is a tearoom and toilets. Shelters with seats are provided at convenient intervals along the promenade, which has much more the air of a seaside resort than a capital city.

Continue, with parkland grazed by cattle on the left, to Cramond Point (more toilets). Cramond Tower, on the left, was originally built in the 15th century for the Bishops of Dunkeld. It is worth walking up Cramond Glebe Road past the car park for the short distance to see Cramond Kirk. The tower, the oldest part, is 15th century. The main part was completed in 1656. A drink at a riverside pub or cafe will round off this very pleasing walk in style.

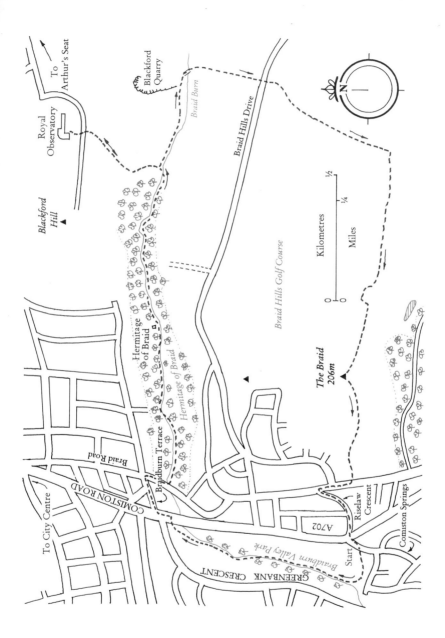

THE BRAID HILLS

This very varied and interesting walk offers a quiet glen, a ridge with superb views – and a chance to see the stars.

The walk starts by taking the gate about 100 m down Comiston Springs Avenue on the right, into Braidburn Valley Park. Curve round to the right with the path and walk along beside the burn under an avenue of trees. The park is largely open and grassed and provides a safe play and exercise area for both children and dogs.

Walk along to the end of the park and leave it by the gate into Greenbank Crescent. Cross Comiston Road into Braidburn Terrace, cross Braid Road and turn right. In 100 m turn left into Hermitage of Braid, taking the broad main path to rejoin the Braid Burn. Just before the stable block is reached, a brick structure is seen in the burn. This was a water pumping device which supplied water to the house, which is itself reached about 200 m further on. Up on the hillside to the left (not visible from the path) is a large dovecot with 1985 boxes. Dovecots were very important in former times as the birds provided a supply of meat.

A stone outside the house records that the Hermitage was gifted to the City of Edinburgh by John McDougal, and opened as a park on 10 June 1938 by the then Lord Provost, Sir Louis Gumley. The area is thought to take its name from one Henri de Brad, who owned the land here in the 12th century, and was also Sheriff of Edinburgh.

The present house dates to 1785, when it was built for Charles Gordon of Cluny, who had bought the estate in 1772. It is in baronial style with turrets and mock battlements. The architect may have been Robert Burn. The house is now the headquarters of the Edinburgh District Council countryside ranger service, and is open to visitors. It contains interesting displays and information about the area and other parts of Edinburgh's countryside.

INFORMATION

Distance: 10 km (6 miles).

Start and finish: Comiston Springs Avenue, off Comiston Road. Leave City Bypass at A702 turnoff, turn left, go straight over at Fairmilehead traffic lights, and Comiston Springs Avenue is then the fifth road on the left. From the city centre follow A702 signs along Morningside Road into Comiston Road and go right into Comiston Springs Avenue where the road bends left.

Terrain: Roads and good paths. No special footwear needed.

Public transport: Buses LRT 11, 15 (not Sunday), 24 (not Sunday), SMT 100, 101, WIL 103 from city centre to Comiston Road.

Refreshments: The Blackstone pub/bistro and the Braid Hills Hotel are near the start. Tearoom at Hermitage of Braid open on Sundays only, April to September, 1100–1730.

Opening hours:
Hermitage of Braid Visitor Centre: Mon-Fri 1000–1600, Sun (April-Sept only) 1100–1800. *Royal Observatory:* Open daily. April-Sept 1200–1730; Oct-Mar 1300–1700 (admission charge).

Hermitage of Braid.

Continue on the main path, pausing to look at the icehouse on the slope opposite the house, a way of keeping provisions fresh in the days before refrigerators. The path carries on down the glen, which is very steep sided, heavily wooded with many fine trees, and can be quite dark even in summer. Between two bridges over the burn are a number of amusingly carved wooden beasts and fish.

Cross the burn for the third time and reach the end of the trees. If you wish to enjoy Blackford Hill and the Observatory, take the steps on the left just after going under the wooden bridge. Continue climbing on the path and after about 100 m take the first obvious path to the right which slants up to join another stony path climbing the hill.

Horses graze beside the Braid Burn.

At an open grassy area go half left between banks of gorse up to a seat and continue ahead to the Royal Observatory, established here just 100 years ago in 1894. There is a splendid view of Arthur's Seat and down the Firth to the east. The attractions at the Observatory include very interesting exhibitions on astronomy, including one marking its centenary, and the chance to view the heavens through powerful telescopes.

To continue the walk, return to the bridge over the Braid Burn and turn left. Across the burn you may see horses grazing the field. Pass the high rock faces of

Blackford Quarry. It was here that the Swiss geologist Agassiz (1807–73) made pioneering observations on the passage of glaciers across the land. A plaque commemorating him has been placed by the quarries, but is not passed on this walk.

About 500 m from the Braid Burn bridge, go right over another bridge (signed Howe Dean Path) and through a kissing gate. The path climbs steadily up a wooded gully and leads to a long flight of wooden steps. At the top, cross Braid Hills Road and continue on the path across the golf course. Cross the 10th hole near the green, then pass the 11th tee. When the clear path ends, go straight ahead until you reach a broad track by a stone dyke. You cross several more holes; keep a wary lookout for golfers who may be playing in your direction.

Turn right by the dyke and walk along the track, climbing gradually to the triangulation pillar marking the summit of the Braid Hills, passing a large radio mast of the kind which seem to crown so many hills nowadays. Just before the mast, beware of golfers driving off from a tee just above your head to the left!

The view from the summit is magnificent. It extends through 360 degrees and from east to west takes in Berwick Law and the Bass Rock, the Firth, Arthur's Seat and the city centre, the castle, Corstorphine Hill, the bridges, the Fife and Ochil Hills, and right round behind you to Caerketton and Allermuir. Truly a view worth savouring.

From the summit the path drops steeply down to emerge on Braid Road. Cross and turn right then take the first left (Riselaw Crescent). Cross Comiston Road to return to Comiston Springs Avenue at the end of what must be one of the most satisfying walks to be found in any city. An interesting footnote is that Edinburgh's first piped water supply was taken from the springs at Comiston as long ago as 1681. The springs were named Hare, Fox, Teuchat (Lapwing) and Swan. The original water storage house still exists not far away in Oxgangs Loan.

THE WATER OF LEITH 2: BALERNO TO SLATEFORD

This section of the Water of Leith Walkway goes from Balerno, on the city's edge, to Slateford. Despite the increasingly urban nature of the surrounding areas, it maintains a pleasantly rural feel, keeping generally close to the water. For much of the way the path uses a former railway track.

Leave Balerno by Bridge Road. On the right is the entrance to Malleny House, a 17th century mansion built for Sir James Murray of Kilbaberton. The house and grounds were gifted to the National Trust for Scotland by Mrs Gore-Browne Henderson in 1968. The house is privately occupied, but the splendid walled garden is open every day. It contains fine roses, and Scotland's national collection of Bonsai (miniature trees), but is perhaps most notable for its magnificent clipped yews. There are four left of an original group known as the Twelve Apostles, said to have been planted to mark the Union of the Crowns in 1603.

INFORMATION

Distance: 9 km (5.5 miles).

Start: Balerno (several free car parks).

Finish: Slateford.

Terrain: Paths and roads. Paths can be muddy in wet weather. Strong footwear advised.

Public transport: Buses LRT 43, 44 (daily), SMT 44, 66 (not Sundays) from city centre to Balerno, passing through Slateford.

Opening hours: *Malleny House Garden:* All year, daily 0930–sunset.

Clipped yews in Malleny House Garden.

The Water of Leith
near Currie.

Cross the bridge over the Water of Leith and in 150m
turn right at the encouraging sign 'Public Path to
Slateford'. The path drops down to the water, with the
grounds of Currie Rugby Club on the far bank. The
high retaining wall of the road is to the left, with a
large pigeon loft filled with stones instead of birds!

Follow the old railway, which was known to local
people as the Balerno Express before its closure in
1968, as it winds along beside the river, which is quite
fast-flowing after rain. The Water of Leith rises from
Harperrig Reservoir in the Pentlands.

In 800 m the path passes Kinauld Farm, on the site of
a waulk mill. There were numerous mills all along the
course of the river, prooducing cloth, flour and paper.
The path crosses the river, and passes the large former
Balerno Paper Mill, now a tannery.

Before long, on the right, is another high retaining
wall. This was the training ground for the youthful
Dougal Haston, a Currie lad who went on to become
the first Scot to climb Mount Everest. On the opposite
bank you see Currie Bowling Club, founded in 1875.
There are seats at regular intervals along the path if
you feel like a pause to contemplate the trees and the
rushing water. Through the trees you may be able to

glimpse the ruin of Lennox Tower, a 15th century stronghold said to have been a favourite hunting place of James VI.

The path crosses above Kirkgate, but it is worth leaving it to look at Currie Kirk, on the right. Currie was once called Killeith – 'the chapel by the Leith'. The present church was begun in 1785, to a design by James Thomson. The clock was added in 1818. The parish records include some notable examples of longevity, including one William Napier, who lived to be 113. Next to the church, the ruined choir of the old church has been turned into a meeting hall as a memorial to Rev David Stewart, minister here for 52 years from 1898 to 1950.

Return to the railway path and continue, passing a weir and shortly afterwards crossing Kinleith Burn, called the 'Poet's Burn', after James Thomson, the 'Weaver Poet', who lived hereabouts achieved some fame in the early 19th century. The burn runs down the 'Poet's Glen', met again in walk14.

A path on the right leads to the charmingly-named Blinkbonny. Carry on along the riverside path, passing through a rather drab industrial area before meeting the river again. Pass under a road bridge and by a neat cottage, with a large coup behind it, then cross the river to enter Juniper Green. One of the mills here produced snuff from 1749 to 1920.

The name Juniper Green first appears on 18th century maps and may simply have come from the prevailing shrub cover of junipers. In 1896, one John Geddie wrote that 'townspeople find Juniper Green a pleasant and acceptable retreat all the year round'. It is now a suburb of Edinburgh, but retains its countryside links not least through the river and its path.

In a further 800 m, the scenery opens out nicely as the path joins a minor road, before leaving it at the Splash bathworks. The city bypass can be heard ahead, and then seen. Cross the access road to the mill of Alexander Inglis, grain merchants and rejoin the riverside path. Go under the bypass and pass a weir as the river curves sharply right.

The path crosses the river twice in quick succession, briefly joining a minor road before turning left into Spylaw Park. You may see squirrels darting around in here. Pass under Bridge Road, then reach a small car park at the former Colinton Station. The path then passes through a tunnel – there are lights – to enter Colinton Dell, a pleasant wooded section of the river valley.

Above the dell on the east is Merchiston Castle School. In its grounds are the remains of the 17th century Colinton Castle. The next section needs a little care as there are several branch or cross paths which can be confusing. In 400 m go right, down the second set of steps, and cross the river at a weir. Cross a lade and go up steps to a road. Cross the road, go left round a house and rejoin the riverside path, which can be rather muddy along this stretch.

At a bridge (Bogmill Road) keep the river on your left and go round a right-hand bend to enter Craiglockhart Dell. Pass a neat wooden footbridge and continue past a 19th century grotto, formerly in the grounds of Craiglockhart House.

In a further 400 m, the path emerges onto Slateford Road right by the Tickled Trout pub. The bus stop for Balerno is outside the pub and there are four or five services per hour, so you should not have to wait long. Across the road are the offices of the Water of Leith Conservation Trust (mornings only), where you can see, and buy, further material on the river and its path.

Just ahead of you are two splendid pieces of civil engineering. The Slateford Aqueduct (Hugh Baird, 1822) carries the Union Canal over the river on eight arches, and John Miller's railway viaduct, built 20 years later, strides across in 14 grand steps.

After this walk I am sure you will agree with the world's best bad poet, William Topaz McGonagall, who in his inimitable style enthused:

Autumn colouring by the waterside.

Therefore all lovers of the picturesque be advised by me
And the beautiful scenery of the River of Leith go and see,
And I am sure you will get a very great treat
Because the River of Leith scenery cannot be beat.

If the construction of this verse leaves something to be desired, the spirit of its words is perfect.

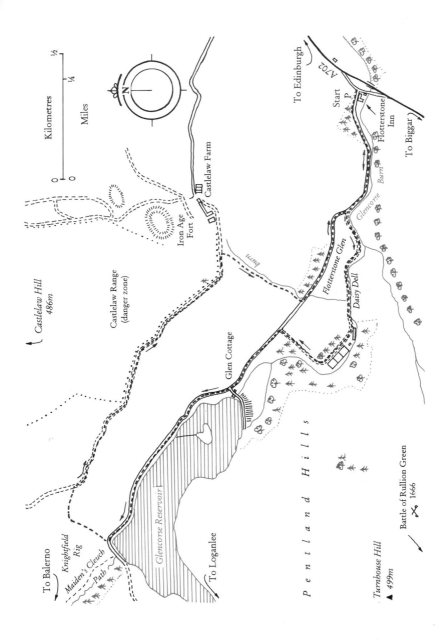

Castlelaw Hill
486m

Castlelaw Range
(danger zone)

Castlelaw Farm

Iron Age
Fort

burn

To Edinburgh

Start

P

Flotterstone
Inn

A702

To Biggar

Barn

Glencorse

Flotterstone Glen

Daisy Dell

Glen Cottage

Glencorse Reservoir

To Loganlee

To Balerno

Knightfield
Rig

Maiden's Cleuch
Path

P e n t l a n d   H i l l s

Turnhouse Hill
▲ 499m

Battle of Rullion Green
1666

Kilometres

Miles

½

¼

0

N

Climb up beside the plantation and at the top, cross the stile and turn right on the clear track. From here there is a splendid view down the length of Glencorse Reservoir to Loganlea, with Turnhouse Hill to the left.

Walk along the track, with views ahead extending to the Moorfoot Hills. To the left, marked by red and white posts, is the Castlelaw Range, part of the 800 hectares owned by the Ministry of Defence and used for training. Go through a gateway and swing right then left. The track has now acquired a rough surface. Behind and to the left, below the screes of Castlelaw Hill, is an artillery range. When not in use, sheep graze unconcernedly over it.

At a building where the track swings left, just before Castlelaw Farm, go right (signposted 'Glencorse'). A slight detour, ahead, around the farm leads to a car park from which an Iron Age fort is signposted. Your direction however is back down to the road. For the first 50 m there is no clear path. Keep well above the burn to the left and a path soon appears, left of a dyke.

Follow the path down to the road and turn left to return to Flotterstone. This whole area was much loved by R. L. Stevenson, and little wonder, for it is beautiful at all times of the year. In his later years, exiled in Samoa, Stevenson wrote to his fellow author S. R. Crockett that 'the dearest burn to me in the world is that which drums and pours in cunning wimples in that glen of yours behind Glencorse old kirk . . . Go there and say a prayer for me'. In the heat of the South Seas he found that 'my imagination continually inhabits the cold old huddle of grey hills from which we came'. Stevenson was never to see those hills again, but his spirit is much with us as we walk in the Pentlands today.

Ducks beside the reservoir.

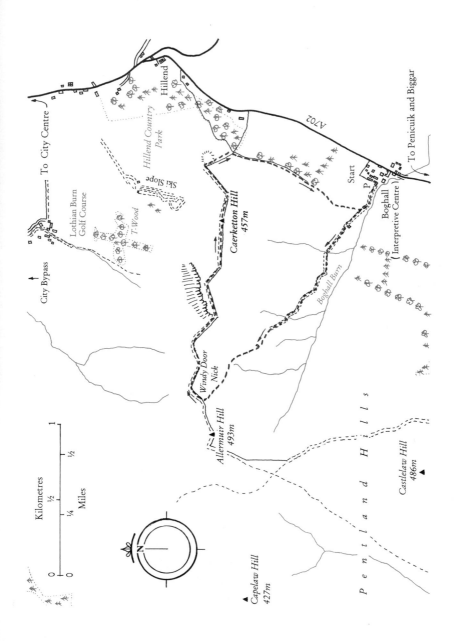

CAERKETTON HILL

This delightful walk serves as an excellent introduction to the Pentland Hills and gives an incomparable panorama of the whole city of Edinburgh. Before you start, do take the time to look round the interpretive centre at Boghall, which has information and displays on the land use in the area and on the Pentland Hills Regional Park, whose headquarters the fine principal building is. Boghall is a demonstration and research farm run by Scottish Agricultural College (SAC).

Start the walk from the car park by following the 'Farm Trail' sign. The fenced path with a woodbark surface winds round the back of the farm. Cross a track (footpath sign ahead) and pause at the interpretive board for Boghall Pond on the left, originally a source of water power for a nearby grain mill.

Cross Boghall Burn and turn right up steps, passing another interpretive board with information on the small gorge which has many old beech trees and conifers. Treecreepers are among the birds that may be spotted here, and the plants include herb robert, dog violet, primrose, wood sorrel and celandine.

Go right with the path to recross the burn and up steps to a sign 'footpath to Hillend and Allermuir'. Go left here, along the track, through a gate towards the open

Dog Violet

INFORMATION

Distance: 6 km (4 miles).

Start and finish: Boghall Farm, on A702 3 km (2 miles) south of the City Bypass.

Public transport: Buses from the city centre to Penicuik or Biggar (SMT/WES 100, 101, WIL 103) pass Boghall.

Terrain: Good paths and tracks. Gradual climb, steep descent. Boots or strong footwear advised.

Refreshments: None en route. Nearest at Hillend.

Opening hours: *Boghall Farm Interpretive Centre:* Monday-Friday, 1000–1200, 1300–1600. Closed at weekends.

The panoramic view from Caerketton.

hill, with Capelaw Hill ahead and Castlelaw, part of the military range, to the left.

Continue on the track which climbs steadily before levelling out and passing through two gates (usually open). The track winds on round the hill with wide views looking back across the plain to the Moorfoot Hills. Cross a stile: your first objective – the col between Allermuir and Caerketton – is now clear ahead and to the right.

Cross two more stiles to leave the inbye land behind. Another interpretive board tells of the 17th century farming method of 'ridge and furrow' which was practised here. At a path junction go left (yellow arrow). There are hardy blackface sheep on the hill, some heather among the grasses and also small patches of juniper scrub.

The path takes an economical line round the hill and up to the col, which bears the delightful name of Windy Door Nick. Cross the stile: the view of Edinburgh and the Firth of Forth now begins to open up. If you wish to climb Allermuir, it is a short diversion to the left, adding about half an hour to the walk.

Otherwise, turn right on the clear path up Caerketton. As you climb you get a great view of the main Pentland ridge behind you to the south. Keep by the fence to the summit, where the panorama ahead will make you stop dead in your tracks. Directly below is Lothianburn golf course and the aptly named T-Wood. Traffic roars along the City Bypass, with Edinburgh spread out in plan beyond it, and the skyline extending from Grangemouth in the west to Bass Rock and Berwick Law in the east. To the north, across the Firth, the hills of Fife are clear. Little wonder R. L. Stevenson ached for this view when he was far away on a Pacific island, writing that 'using that inward eye which is the bliss of solitude . . . I, from Halkerside, from topmost Allermuir, or steep Caerketton, dreaming, gaze again'. It is a wonderful place to have just outside a city.

When you have drunk your fill of the view, leave by continuing along the fence. Pass over a subsidiary summit and begin to descend, steadily at first and then very steeply (take care here). Looking left, you can see Hillend and the artificial ski slope.

Looking out over the city with the T-wood in the foreground.

Keep by the fence to a stile at the foot of the steep slope. Turn right here and follow the path by the fence, with an extensive area of gorse, bright yellow in spring, to the left. At the cross fence, turn right over the stile (yellow arrow) and follow the fence along above the shelter belt. There may be some boggy stretches along here.

The path meanders across towards Boghall, maintaining the same height. After leaving the wood, keep ahead to cross a stile and walk just above the fence, left of the tall wooden mast, and down to the main track. Turn left, back to the farm and the car park. The masts were a 1950s aerial for a radio telescope for Sir Edward Appleton, the famous astronomer who late became Principal of Edinburgh University.

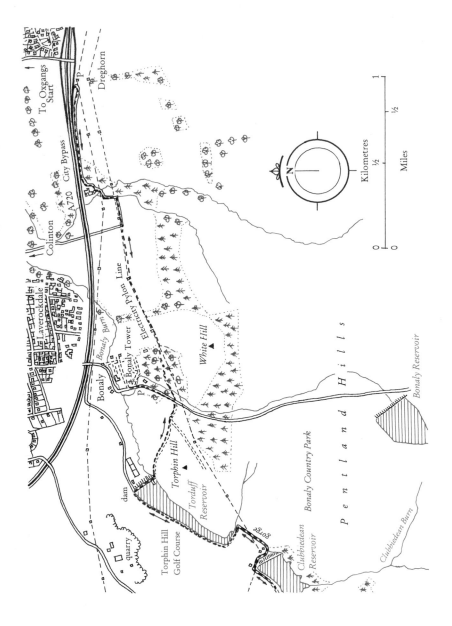

DREGHORN TO BONALY

This walk uses a path recently opened by agreement with the Ministry of Defence between the small car park at Dreghorn, right by the city bypass, and Bonaly Country Park, giving an unusual approach to Bonaly and a satisfying walk which takes in two more of the Pentland reservoirs.

From the car park, continue along the access road and go through a gate, using a wicket gate at its right hand side. Just a few metres to your right the traffic on the bypass roars unceasingly along. Swing left past a boarded-up house and continue along the road, the traffic noise now receding, no doubt to your relief.

At a field corner, a fingerpost points to Bonaly. At the next corner, where the road swings right, leave it and go through the wicket gate into the field. Keep the fence and hedge on your right for the next 200 m, when you will see another fingerpost pointing right to Laverockdale (laverock is the Scots word for a skylark) and ahead to Bonaly.

Follow the overhead power line across the field, going slightly uphill, to reach and cross a stile. Continue following the pylon line, now following a clear path. At a fork, go left on a delightful path which climbs to give a splendid view back across the city.

The path runs round above a plantation of mixed woodland and broadens. Keep near to the fence and

INFORMATION

Distance: 10 km (6 miles).

Start and finish: Dreghorn car park. Take the Colinton turnoff from the City Bypass (no road number) and from the westbound offramp on the south side, go left and right into the car parking area.

Terrain: Road and hill paths. Strong footwear advised especially in wet conditions.

Public transport: Buses to Oxgangs (LRT 5, 17, 51) or Hunter's Tryst (LRT 16, SMT C11) then a short walk to the start.

Refreshments: None en route.

The flowery path to Bonaly.

drop down. Cross a flatter area and then go right, down steps, across a small burn, up steps and along to the information board beside Bonaly car park. Turn left on the path (across the main track). A short climb gives another fine view over the city. Nearer to hand, Bonaly Tower peeps out of the wood. The tower was extended from the original farmhouse by Lord Cockburn, who had purchased the estate in 1811.

Torduff Reservoir.

He too enjoyed wandering the Pentlands, writing in his Memorials that 'There is not a recess in the valleys of the Pentlands, nor an eminence on their summits, that is not familiar to my solitude. One summer I read every word of Tacitus in the sheltered crevice of a rock about 800 feet above the level of the sea, with the most magnificent of scenes before me'. That scene is still presented to us today; though it is much altered from Lord Cockburn's time, we can appreciate why he said 'There are few landscapes more beautiful or more varied'.

Keep right at a fork and walk along by the fence to reach Torduff Reservoir. Ahead, golfers playing the Torphin Hill course can be seen. The path continues across the dam and along the far side of Torduff, one of the smaller Pentland reservoirs. It was completed in 1851 and has a maximum depth of 22 m and a capacity of 110 million gallons. From the dam there is another very fine view taking in Arthur's Seat, the castle and out across the Firth.

The walk continues along the access road to Clubbiedean. At the end of Torduff, which sits deep in a narrow glen, the road swings left and crosses the miniature gorge carrying the burn linking the two reservoirs. It then swings right again and climbs to

Clubbiedean Reservoir.

Clubbiedean, which was completed in 1850, a year before Torduff. At its south-west end are the remains of a prehistoric fort. Clubbiedean is stocked as a trout fishery.

The return to Dreghorn is by the outward route. Although there are many fine walks in Bonaly, few of them are circular, and there is no access westward from Clubbiedean to link up with the routes which go through the hills from Dreghorn. The Regional Park Service is however looking at ways in which links can be developed

Returning by the same path is no hardship, however; the views are always different the other way around, and pleasant spots noted on the way across can perhaps be explored in more detail on the return. These may include the burn leading down and under the bypass to Laverockdale, a very pleasant area of woodland.

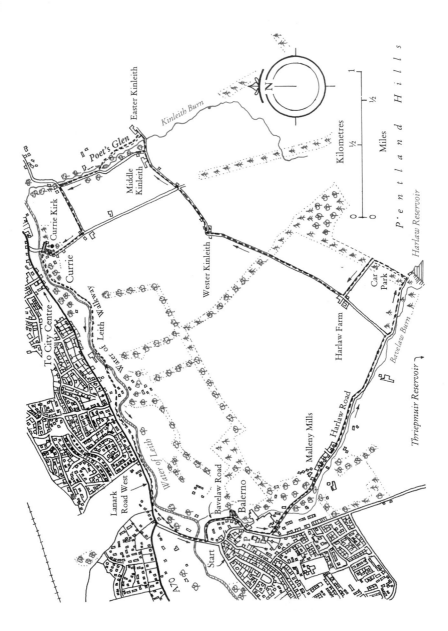

HARLAW AND THE POET'S GLEN

This walk might be called 'the Pentland fringe'. It approaches Edinburgh's hill range but does not rise into them, keeping instead to the lower ground and skirting one of the area's many reservoirs. It makes a very pleasant afternoon outing.

From the car park, turn right into Bavelaw Road. Buses pass along this road. Turn left into Harlaw Road, and follow it as it crosses the Bavelaw Burn. The burn rises high on East Cairn Hill in the Pentlands, but much of its original early course now lies beneath Thriepmuir and Harlaw Reservoirs. Above the former is Bavelaw Castle, a 17th century stronghold of the Scotts of Harperrig. It is said that King James VI and I hunted here.

Continue up the road, passing houses built by the former papermill company in Balerno and a wood apparently owned by the Save the Children Fund. After this on the right are the buildings of the former Malleny Mills, no longer operating.

About 800 m from Balerno, where the road turns sharply left, go right onto a footpath. This rather secretive little path runs along high above the Bavelaw Burn through a dense wood and in 500 m reaches another road. Go ahead here past a cottage to reach Harlaw reservoir.

INFORMATION

Distance: 9 km (5.5 miles).

Start and finish: Balerno. Park in the Bavelaw car park on Bavelaw Road.

Terrain: Roads and good paths. No special footwear needed.

Public transport: Buses LRT 43, 44 (daily), SMT 44, 66 (not Sundays) (Sunday SMT 66A) from city centre to Balerno, passing through Currie.

Refreshments: Pubs and cafes in Balerno and Currie.

Harlaw reservoir.

Harlaw and its companion to the west, Thriepmuir, were constructed in 1847–48 as part of the large-scale works to supply the ever-growing population of Edinburgh with clean water. In a dozen years, seven substantial reservoirs were provided around the Pentlands, starting with these two and ending with Harperrig. They are all now well used for recreation including walking, fishing and sailing, and birdlife is plentiful on most of them.

The sharp little peak on the right skyline is West Kip. The walk can be extended by 2 km by continuing right round Harlaw. Otherwise, return to the road and walk along it. At the car park, turn left, down to Harlaw Farm. Turn right and walk along this quiet road. As you near Wester Kinleith, there is a grand view across much of Edinburgh. Kinleith was originally 'Killeith', the chapel of the Water of Leith, and the name encompassed Currie as well.

Continue to the next junction, and go straight across (marked no through road for cars). There are again good views of the city. Go through Middle Kinleith, and just past the main block of buildings divert down a lane to the left. A cottage here, called Mount Parnassus, was the home of the 'weaver poet' James Thomson.

The pond in the Poet's Glen, an idyllic spot.

Go back to the road, turn left over the bridge, and just before a 'private road' sign at Easter Kinleith, take a path on the left which leads into the glen of Kinleith Burn, called 'the poet's glen' after Thomson. Don't go down the tempting steps on the left: they lead down to Kinleith Burn, but not much further. Instead continue on the path, and at a fork go left to reach a hidden little pool where it is said the poet often came to contemplate nature. A heron may be seen fishing here (his spirit, perhaps) and it seems that somewhere in the undergrowth is a stone inscribed with a verse of Thomson's poetry.

Cross a little bridge and then a stile to continue outside a high wall, which hides the burn and its deep wee glen, and the poet's secrets, from the eyes. Cross another stile and continue down to the road. Turn left and in 300 m go right to walk down towards Currie.

At a gate turn right into the kirkyard, which has many interesting memorials. On the left is the mausoleum of Sir Stanley Davidson, who died in 1981 aged 87 after a distinguished medical career. He was Regius Professor of Medicine at both

Currie Kirk.

Aberdeen and Edinburgh Universities and from 1953–57 was president of the Royal College of Physicians of Edinburgh.

Walk round to the front of the church (for a fuller description see walk 10), and down the steps to the road. Turn right, go under the bridge and immediately go right up steps to gain the Water of Leith Walkway, which is followed back to Balerno, reversing the route taken in walk 10.

If you wish to shorten the walk, you can continue into Currie and take one of the frequent buses back to Balerno.

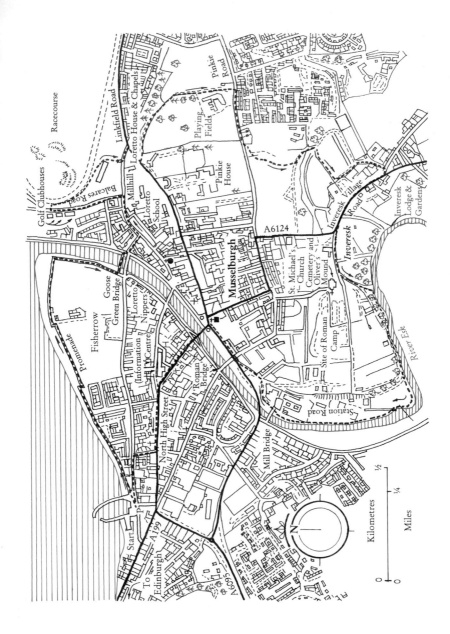

MUSSELBURGH AND INVERESK

Musselburgh's nickname is 'the Honest Toun', earned in the 14th century when its citizens refused a reward for caring for the body of the Earl of Moray after he died here. The names Musselburgh and Fisherrow indicate that the town once looked to the sea for its living. There has been a harbour here since Roman times. In medieval times Fisherrow was an important port handling salt and coal and building boats, as well as having a large fishing fleet. Today it is mainly used by yachts, many of which you will see as you start the walk by turning onto the Promenade, heading east.

When the tide is out there are extensive mudflats here, with wading birds busily picking away at delicacies. There is also a lovely view in both directions, east along the Firth and back to Edinburgh with (of course) Arthur's Seat prominent.

At the end of the houses, jink right and left with the path, cross Fisherrow Links and then jink left and right. Follow the path round the wall of a pumping station to reach the outflow of the River Esk. Turn right along the river alongside the Loretto playing fields, towards Goose Green Bridge.

INFORMATION

Distance: 8 km (5 miles).

Start and finish: Car park, Fisherrow harbour.

Terrain: Roads and good paths. No special footwear needed.

Public transport: Buses LRT 15, 26, 43, 44, 85, 86, LOW 104, 128, SMT 44, 66, 129 from Edinburgh to Musselburgh (Sunday services 26A, 43A, 44, 104, 128. SMT 66A). Alight at North High Street and walk down to the harbour. Also regular trains from Edinburgh to Musselburgh, though the station is some way from the town.

Refreshments: Good selection of pubs and cafes in the town.

Opening hours: *Inveresk Lodge Gardens:* All year. Mon-Fri 1000–1600, Sun 1400–1700. Plus April-Oct, Sat 1400–1700. Admission charge. Tourist Information Centre, *Brunton Hall:* Apr-Sept, daily 1000–1700. Tel: 0131 665 6597.

Distant Arthur's Seat from Fisherrow.

Cross the bridge, go ahead into James Street and then left into Millhill. Many of the buildings here belong to Loretto School. The distinctive building at the corner of Millhill Lane is the Colin Thomson Hall, designed in 1935 by John Matthew. Diagonally opposite is Trafalgar House. Built in 1812 and once owned by a sea-captain who fought with Nelson at Trafalgar, it is now Loretto's girls' boarding-house.

Turn left into Balcarres Road. This short diversion enables you to see four golf clubhouses, of which the second is the grandest. It belonged to the Honourable Company of Edinburgh Golfers, the oldest golf club in Scotland, founded in the 1740s. The building dates from 1865, but in 1891 the club moved to its present home at Muirfield (walk 17). The fourth clubhouse originally served the Royal Burgess club, but after many years in other use was recently acquired by Musselburgh Old Course Club as its headquarters.

From here, provided there is no racing taking place, it is usually possible to walk across the racecourse ahead of you to the golf car park and thus back out to Millhill. Otherwise, return by the road. Golf and racing have shared these links for a very long time. Golf has been played at Musselburgh for over 400 years, and the Open Championship was held here several times in the 19th century. Racing has taken place since 1817. The two sports seem to coexist quite happily.

Continue along Millhill to Linkfield Road, cross with care and turn right. On the corner is Loretto House, where Dr Thomas Langhorne founded the famous school (at that time for boys only) in 1827. The building is still in use. In its grounds are the scant remains of Loretto Chapel, where in 1543 Mary of Guise, mother of Mary, Queen of Scots, came to pray for peace with England. To no avail: the chapel was sacked by Hertford's troops the following year. The school took its name from the chapel, which in turn was named for a town in Italy said to hold items associated with the Virgin Mary.

Turn left through gates into the Pinkie playing fields and follow the path round to the left and then curving right, past a large doocot. It dates from the early 17th century and over one door are the intertwined initials of Sir Alexander Seton and his bride Mary Hay. Birds still use the building.

Leave the park beside Pinkie St Peter's primary school, cross Pinkie Road and turn right. Over to the right can be seen Pinkie House. The oldest part is a 16th century tower, round which was built Sir Alexander Seton's large 17th century mansion. It has a notable painted ceiling, which can occasionally be viewed (enquire locally). The house was acquired by the Hopes of Craighall in 1788, and since 1951 has been part of Loretto.

Turn left into Park Lane. At its end go right on a path into Lewisvale Park. In 150 m go left up a narrow stepped path between hedges. Follow the path as it curves round the large open area above. At the far corner, leave the park along Double Dykes – well-named, it has indeed two substantial walls – and at its end cross Inveresk Village Road to see Inveresk Lodge Garden.

The 17th century lodge (not open) and its lovely terraced garden were presented to the National Trust for Scotland in 1959 by Mrs Helen Brunton. The garden has splendid roses and is a very attractive and peaceful place at all times of the year.

St Michael's Church.

After viewing the garden continue along the road, passing a number of fine houses. At a sharp right-hand bend go straight on (no through road sign) to reach the imposing St Michael's Church and Inveresk Cemetery. The church, on the site of an earlier foundation, dates from 1805.

Near its main door is the tomb of Major William Ramsay of the Royal Horse Artillery, who fought in a number of campaigns and fell at the Battle of Waterloo in 1815, aged 33. The stone records that his brother Alexander was killed 'in the Batteries before

The Ramsay tomb.

New Orleans' in the same year, aged just 23. Also buried here is their father, Captain David Ramsay RN, who outlived his sons by three years. Many members of the Hope family of Craighall and Pinkie House also rest here.

West of the church is Oliver's Mound, where Cromwell's troops mounted a cannon. You can see why: it commands a splendid view of Edinburgh and the town of Musselburgh below. West again, in the next field, there was a substantial Roman garrison, at the northern end of Dere Street, which comes all the way from the Border, south of Jedburgh.

Near the mound is another intriguing stone with an elaborate inscription to the Reverend James Scott, who died in 1793 aged just 21. It was 'erected by his disconsolate congregation as a testimony to their sincere respect', so the young minister clearly made his mark.

Leave the church and go down the lane opposite (signed to the River Esk Walkway). Turn right along the riverside path, which is very pleasant with many trees, although the river is rather hidden at first.

River and path swing sharply right back towards the town and pass a weir. On the high ground across the river, the Scottish army under the Earl of Arran took up position in September 1547 to face the Duke of Somerset's troops at the Battle of Pinkie, one of the many skirmishes of the 'Rough Wooing'. Instead of holding their good defensive position, the Scots advanced on the English forces over the old bridge (see below) and were routed; an estimated 10,000 lives were lost and the day became known as Black Saturday.

The path joins Station Road. The railway now passes well south of Musselburgh but there was indeed once a station here, near the centre of town: the road bridge ahead originally carried the trains. The steel footbridge, known as the Mill Bridge, was built in 1923 to take workers to the mills on your right. Paper was made here, and it was also Scotland's main production centre of nets for the fishing industry. The company involved, J. & W. Stuart, made anti-submarine nets during both World Wars. The former Net Mill is now an elegant office building.

The Esk in Musselburgh.

Go up steps, cross the road and continue along the riverside path to the 'Roman Bridge', which is actually medieval, though it may well be on the line of a Roman road. This was the bridge used by the Scottish troops at the Battle of Pinkie. Carry on past the statue of David Macbeth Moir, poet and physician, and go under the main road bridge, a Rennie design of 1806.

Continue beside the river to a footbridge. Cross and walk along North High Street, passing Loretto Junior School – for the Nippers, says its notice! Pass behind the Brunton Hall, often used for concerts and plays, turn right through the Gracefield car park and at the road end turn left to return to the harbour at the end of a varied and satisfying walk.

Pleasure yachts in Musselburgh harbour.

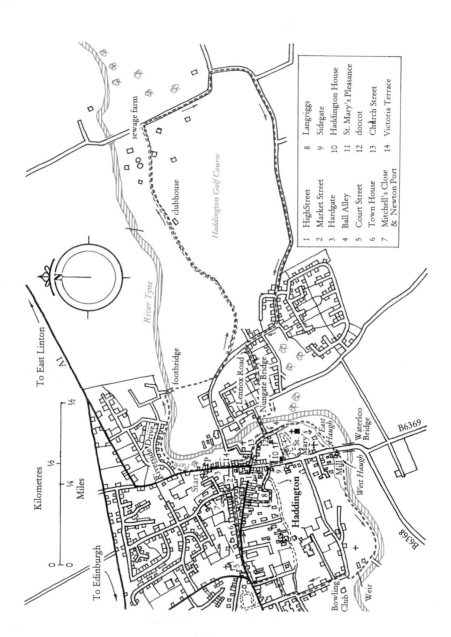

Key

1	HighStreet	8	Langriggs
2	Market Street	9	Sidegate
3	Hardgate	10	Haddington House
4	Ball Alley	11	St. Mary's Pleasance
5	Court Street	12	doocot
6	Town House	13	Church Street
7	Mitchell's Close & Newton Port	14	Victoria Terrace

HADDINGTON

Haddington traces its history back to at least the 12th century, when it became a Royal Burgh. This gave the town the right to trade overseas, most of this trade going through Aberlady, at that time a port. The original burgh was centred around Market Street, High Street and Hardgate, and this central part of Haddington retains much of its character, with many buildings from the 18th and 19th centuries. A walk around the town is indeed a walk through history.

From the car park, walk north up Hardgate and in 250 m turn right on the path leading up to Artillery Park. Turn right into Riverside Drive. Keep on the grass to the right of the houses, and by the children's play area cross the River Tyne by a footbridge. Follow the paved footpath to the road and turn left.

In about 250 m, turn left through imposing gateposts onto Haddington Golf Course. The track across the golf course is a public right of way, but please keep to it and do not stray onto the course itself. It is a pleasant walk much used by local people. The Tyne is across the course to the left.

Once past the clubhouse, continue on a rougher track through a mass of rhododendron bushes. Meet the access road from a sewage farm (often a rather malodorous place!) and continue to the exit gates. Turn right onto the road, at the next junction turn right again, and continue on this road back to Haddington. There is a footpath for most of the way.

Note: If you wish simply to walk around the town, you can miss out this country section.

Back at the entrance to the golf course, cross the road and walk down Lennox Road, its name a reminder that the historic house of Lennoxlove is just south of

INFORMATION

Distance: 6 km
(4 miles).

Start and finish:
Hardgate car park, just north of Market Street.

Terrain: Streets and good paths. No special footwear needed.

Public transport:
Buses LOW/SMT 104 or 106 from Edinburgh to Haddington.

Refreshments:
Selection of cafes and pubs in the town.

Opening hours:
St Mary's Church: Apr-Sep Mon-Sat 1000-1600, Sun 1300–1600. Donations welcome.

Nungate Bridge.

Haddington. The house, home to the Duke and Duchess of Hamilton, was named after a lady known as La Belle Stuart; a mistress of Charles II, she eloped with the Duke of Richmond and Lennox. She is said to have been the model for the figure of Britannia long used on British coins.

At the end of Lennox Road go straight on (Ford Road), then turn right by the river and go up steps to cross the fine old Nungate Bridge. Most of the present bridge is believed to be 16th century, but the two western arches were added in the 18th century.

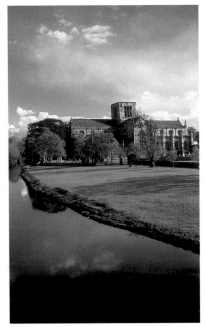

The Tyne and St Mary's Church.

Once across the river, turn left along the Ball Alley – once used for ball games – to reach St Mary's Church. This magnificent building, known as 'the Lamp of Lothian', is one of the largest churches in Scotland. The exterior is richly carved with gargoyles and other figures.

The church was badly damaged in 1548 by Henry VIII's forces. The nave was restored in 1570 under the direction of John Knox, a native of Haddington, but the chancel remained ruined until much more recently. Since 1971 nearly £200,000 has been raised, largely by the Lamp of Lothian Collegiate Trust built up by the Dowager Duchess of Hamilton, who lives at Lennoxlove.

After leaving the church, continue on the riverside path outside the kirkyard wall. Cross a bridge over a lade and continue across East Haugh. Cross the road at Waterloo Bridge and pass Poldrate Mill, a fine 18th century three-storey corn mill which has been renovated for use as a community and arts centre.

Walk across West Haugh by the river. Pass a footbridge and continue until you reach a weir. Leave the path as it bends left and go straight ahead to a road. Continue across playing fields. At the houses, go right and at a bend in 50 metres go straight on along an enclosed path.

Take the first road on the left and walk up to the main road, passing Haddington Bowling Club. Turn right, and right again at the lights, noting on the left the large statue of Robert Ferguson of Raith, MP. The statue was erected by the tenantry of East Lothian in 1843 even though Ferguson was Lord Lieutenant of Fife!

Walk along Court Street, noting the classical police station opposite, to reach the fine Town House at the apex of Market Street and High Street. Built in 1748 to a design of the great William Adam, its 52 m (170 ft) steeple was added in 1831.

Continue along Market Street and turn left into Mitchell's Close. This is the last close of its kind remaining in the town and still shows the medieval pattern, with long low buildings. Mitchell's Close was restored in 1967 and now provides craft workshops as well as houses.

At its end is a modern medical centre. Turn right here, and right again into Newton Port. Cross Market Street and walk down Britannia Wynd, one of a number of narrow lanes or wynds joining the two principal streets. Cross High Street, noting on the left the cross with a goat – the town's symbol – and walk down Ross's Close opposite.

Turn left into Langriggs and right into Sidegate. In 100 m you reach Haddington House on the left. Built in the early 17th century, this is the oldest house in the town. Past the house, turn left into St Mary's Pleasance, a beautiful garden which includes many herbs and other plants common in Scotland in the 17th and 18th centuries.

Walk across the garden to its far lefthand corner, where an almost hidden wooden gate leads out to a path. This in turn leads out by Lady Kitty's Garden past an old doocot into Church Street. Turn left and walk back to Sidegate, on the way passing Elm House (1785) and then St Ann's Place, a lovely enclosed square of buildings. Here too (above the eastern pend) you will find a carving of a goat. No-one seems to know why the animal was adopted as Haddington's symbol or mascot.

Turn right into Sidegate and continue up Hardgate to cross Victoria Terrace and return to the car park.

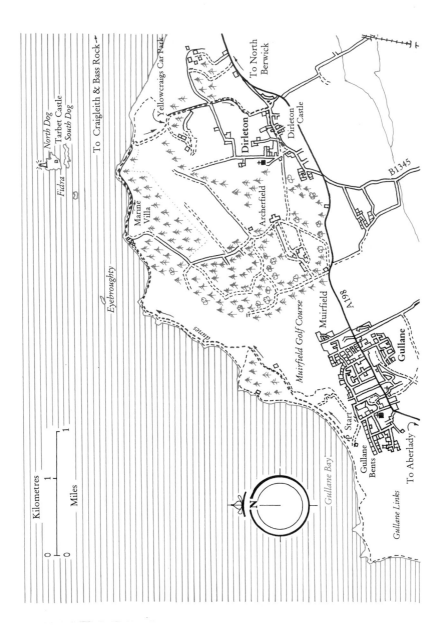

GULLANE AND DIRLETON

The walk starts from the large, informal parking area at Gullane Bents (if arriving by bus, walk down from Gullane). The village of Gullane (pronounced Gillan) is surrounded by golf courses, five in all, and attracts many visiting golfers. The extensive dune system at Gullane Bay has been restored in recent years after being eroded by overuse prewar and then from its use as a practice ground for the 1944 Normandy landings.

From the car park, walk east across the grassy area and continue on a clear gravel track which comes down from the road, following signs to 'overflow car park'. The track narrows to a path which swings left around a plantation. Pass a horseshoe sign and turn right at a white arrow. The path is now very sandy in parts, which makes for hard going.

Wind along between high gorse bushes. At a fork, go right and reach a fence. At another fork, go right again and continue with the fence to swing left along the edge of Muirfield, perhaps the most famous of the golf courses here. This is the home course of the Honourable Company of Edinburgh Golfers, the oldest club in Scotland (see also walk 15). Muirfield is one of the courses regularly used for the Open Championship, at which time it is transformed with grandstands and marquees and there is hardly a bed to be had between here and Edinburgh.

INFORMATION

Distance: 9 km (5.5 miles).

Start: Gullane Bents car park, signposted from A198 in Gullane (fee in summer).

Finish: Dirleton.

Terrain: Paths, tracks and shore. No special footwear needed, but long trousers are advised as protection against prickly undergrowth.

Public transport: Buses LOW/SMT 124, 125 from Edinburgh to Gullane (North Berwick service). The same buses for return from Dirleton.

Opening hours: *Dirleton Castle:* April-Sep Mon-Sat 0930–1830, Sun 1400–1830. Oct-Mar Mon-Sat 0930–1630, Sun 1400–1630. Admission charge.

Fidra.

The path reaches a large green hut. Continue ahead, now on a grassy path, passing a 'footpath to Gullane' sign, and turn left on a clear track beside the links. Go through a gateway and continue on this excellent track, which gives easy walking. When it swings sharply back left, go straight ahead on a rougher path to reach the dunes. The path briefly becomes overgrown: persevere, it doesn't last long.

Continue eastward, the path now clear again and the sea much closer than before to your left. Follow the path towards woodland. Join a track coming up from the shore, and at the edge of the wood, do not go into the trees but go left on a narrow path, briefly following the edge of the wood before striking across open ground.

Reach the wood again very near the shore, by the small islet of Eyebroughty (misspelt Eyebroughy on OS maps). Go down to the shore and walk along the beach or shoreline, with Fidra and its lighthouse very clear ahead and sandstone cliffs to your right.

At the end of the cliffs and the sandy beach, go up a clear path climbing steeply and then levelling out, and continue on this path past a wartime observation post and around the fence of Marine Villa. There is a superb view of Craigleith and Bass Rock ahead, and Fidra is just offshore. There are often many seabirds including rafts of eider ducks to be seen here.

Fidra is actually two small islands, North Dog and South Dog, joined at low tide. At one time it was called Eilbotle, and belonged to the monks of Dryburgh Abbey in the Borders; the remains of a chapel can be seen near the lighthouse.

Continue on the path and across a sandy beach, rounding a point to pick up the path again – and the view of Craigleith and Bass Rock, this time with Berwick Law added to their right. At a fork, go left to keep close to the shore. Rocks here make a good observation point for the birds, especially if you have binoculars with you.

Reach an open area. The presence of many more people indicates that the Yellowcraigs car park is nearby. Head rightward towards the trees to pick up the track from the car park: there are toilets off to the left here.

Go through the car park, where you may find an ice-cream van in summer, and take the footpath beside the road for 1.5 km to reach Dirleton. At the junction, turn right past the Fidra Stores to reach the centre of this, one of the prettiest villages in Scotland with its large green and handsome houses. Dirleton developed in the 17th and 18th centuries and there are still a number of houses from this period, as well as Victorian villas. The Castle Inn is by the noted architect William Burn. Across the green is the Open Arms Hotel and Dirleton Gallery, which has a tearoom.

Dirleton Castle and (below) its gardens.

The main attraction for most people, however, will be Dirleton Castle. It was started in the 13th century by the de Vaux family, wealthy Normans who came to Scotland in the reign of David I, and the original plan was a number of towers connected by a massive curtain wall.

From 1298 to 1311 the castle was in English hands, and it was then taken over by John Halyburton, who had married into the de Vaux family. The castle went by marriage to Lord Ruthven in 1515, and he added a more comfortable living area and a new slated roof. After passing through various hands, Dirleton was attacked and damaged by General Monk's troops in 1650.

It is now cared for by Historic Scotland, and as well as the extensive remains there are beautiful gardens. The castle has a small shop where souvenirs and a guidebook can be purchased. It is hard to believe, looking round the place today, that in June 1649 a number of men and women who had confessed to practising witchcraft were imprisoned here, found guilty, strangled and burned at the stake.

When you have seen round the castle and gardens, walk across the green outside for the short bus journey back to Gullane.

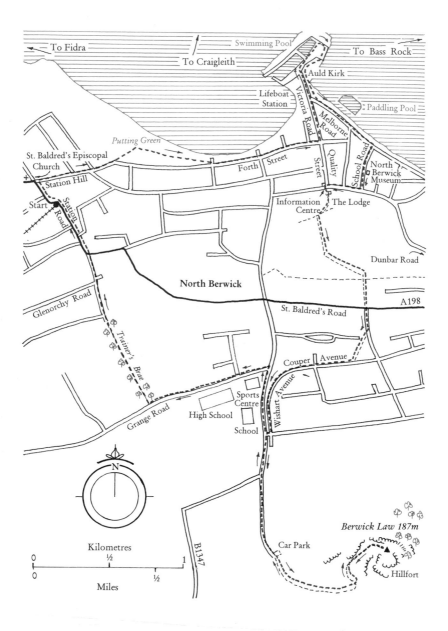

NORTH BERWICK AND THE LAW

Notth Berwick developed as a holiday and golfing resort in the 19th and early 20th century, and continues to be a popular place to live, with many people now commuting to Edinburgh to work.

The walk takes in much of the town and also its most prominent landmark, Berwick Law, which although a mere 187 m (613 ft) in altitude, commands a magnificent panorama because of the lack of higher ground in the area.

From the station, turn left, then right into Station Hill. Opposite is St Baldred's Episcopal Church. Consecrated in 1863, it is dedicated to an 8th century saint who established a monastery at Tyninghame and spent part of his life as a hermit on Bass Rock.

At a fork, keep left and in 100 m go straight on along a tarmac path beside the golf links. The professional's shop is to the left. From here the famous Ben Sayers (1857–1924) established his craft as a maker of golf clubs; the Sayers factory is still here, in Dunbar Road.

Walk along the grass by the shore. There is a good view of Craigleith Island. At the end of the grass area and putting green go along Forth Street and then turn left into Victoria Road (toilets opposite). The lifeboat station, restored and refurbished, was reopened in 1991. Inside is the inflatable Blue Peter III, purchased with help from the enthusiastic viewers of the popular

INFORMATION

Distance: 6.5 km (4 miles).

Start and finish: North Berwick railway station (free car park).

Terrain: Roads, paths and open hill. Strong footwear advised in wet conditions.

Public transport: Regular trains from Edinburgh to North Berwick. Also buses LOW/SMT 124 or 125.

Refreshments: Wide selection of pubs and cafes in North Berwick.

Opening hours: *North Berwick Museum, School Road:* April-September, daily 1100–1700. Admission free. Tel: 01620 895457.
Tourist Information Centre, *Quality Street:* Open all year, 1000-1730. Tel: 01620 892197.

children's TV programme. Continue to the harbour, noting the very large barometer on the wall to the left.

The harbour, where once thousands of barrels of herring were landed, is now home to pleasure craft and just a few fishing boats. Go round to the right, past the open-air swimming pool. These pools were once extremely popular at Scottish resorts, but there are few left open today, their place having been taken by the modern leisure pool with its flumes and wave machines.

Go up steps (by the ladies toilet) and across the grass to the ruins of the Auld Kirk, a 12th century foundation dedicated to St Andrew. Legend states that in 1590, 200 wizards and witches gathered here in a plot devised by the Earl of Bothwell, pretender to the throne, to bring about the downfall of King James VI of Scotland. They used spells and called on the Devil to raise a storm to sink the ship carrying James and his bride, formerly Princess Anne of Denmark, up the Firth to Leith. The plot failed, and James went on to unite the crowns of Scotland and England in 1603.

James VI

Bass Rock.

Continue along Melbourne Road, by the shore, passing a paddling pool, and take the second right (School Road). Here you will find the excellent North Berwick Museum, with displays on Bass Rock, the Law, golf and many other things.

From the museum, continue up School Road and turn right at the junction. Opposite the tourist information centre, turn left through a gate and arch into the grounds of The Lodge. This 18th century building, formerly the town house of the Hamilton-Dalrymple family, was donated by the Town Council to the National Trust for Scotland in 1968.

Take the path behind the house and follow it as it curves right then left. Go ahead past toilets and a play area on a path across the open space, and at a cross path go straight on to leave the park. Your objective, Berwick Law, looms ahead.

Cross St Baldred's Road and walk down Lady Jane Road. Continue on a path and turn right into Couper Avenue, which curves left and becomes Wishart Avenue. At its end go ahead (schools on the right) on the main road and at a bend, go left, signposted for the Law. Pass the car park, go over a stile and turn right on a clear path.

Berwick Law is a scheduled monument. There is evidence of very early occupation on its slopes in the form of ramparts, and at the summit, where there was an Iron Age hillfort. Geologically, it is a 'crag and tail' formation sculpted by retreating ice in just the same way as Castle Rock in Edinburgh.

There are various ways up the Law, all of them steep. As good as any is to continue on the clear path for about 200 m then take the smaller path zigzagging up through gorse to the left. It levels out and curves round the hill, opening up a splendid view inland.

The path swings back left and makes its way up to the summit. Here you will find a view indicator erected in 1959 to the memory of John Wallace Menzies (1889-1956), solicitor and town clerk; a watchtower dating from Napoleonic times, when French invasion was considered a real possibility; a later building used for similar purposes in the two World Wars; and an arch made from a whale's jawbone.

The last-named feature has crowned the hill since at least 1709, and has been replaced several times, most recently in 1936. The most remarkable feature, however, is the view, which takes in much of East Lothian and the Firth of Forth with its islands, the Fife coast and hills, and back to Edinburgh and the Pentlands. It is well worth the effort involved in climbing the hill.

When you are ready to return, retrace your steps to the main road and walk past the Sports Centre. Turn left into Grange Road, passing North Berwick High School on the left. At the end of the houses on the right (Braeside Cottage), turn right along the path known as Trainer's Brae.

This lovely path with fine old trees drops gradually to a lane, at a bend. Go straight ahead and at Glenorchy Road, continue along the same line to reach Station Road and the end of the walk.

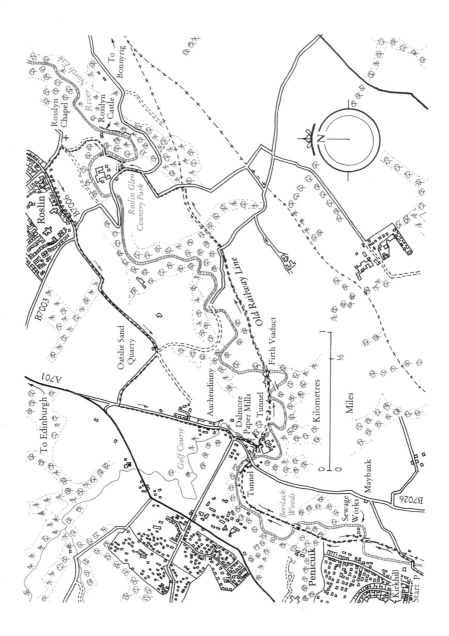

RAILWAY TO ROSLIN

The walk starts from a small parking area best found by taking the B7026 through Auchendinny and in a further 1.5 km turning right at Maybank. This minor road drops down to cross the river and you can park on the right.

From here walk north on the surfaced path following the course of the old railway line to Bonnyrigg, opened in 1872 and closed in 1967. In 400 m the River North Esk is crossed for the first, but by no means the last time. The river is lined with attractive woodland.

Pass a small sewage works and continue, now on a track which goes through Beeslack Woods with numerous paths branching off to either side. There are squirrels in the wood and in summer, many butterflies. The river is crossed again; it loops away to the left and then rejoins the track, chuckling along beside you. The steep bank opposite has been planted with young deciduous trees in protective tubes.

River and track curve sharply to the right, passing the old platform of Auchendinny Station, with Station Cottage to the right. Cross the river for the third time and pass under the road through a short tunnel to reach Dalmore Paper Mills. Take the path between

The North Esk.

INFORMATION

Distance: 9 km (5.5 miles).

Start and finish: Kirkhill, near Penicuik (GR 247607). Alternative start in Roslin.

Terrain: Roads, tracks and paths. No special footwear needed.

Public transport: Buses LOW 62, SMT 64, LRT 81, SMT/WES 100/101, WIL 103, ET 315 (325 on Sunday) from Edinburgh to Penicuik. Short walk down to start. Alternatively, get SMT service 65C or 70 to Roslin and start the circuit there.

Refreshments: Pubs in Roslin and Auchendinny; selection of pubs and cafes in Penicuik.

Opening hours:
Rosslyn Chapel: April-October Mon-Sat 1000–1700, Sun 1200–1645. Admission fee.
Rosslyn Castle: All reasonable hours, free.

fences that runs through the mill and leads beyond it to another tunnel.

Beyond this tunnel the path passes over the splendid ten-arched Firth Viaduct, which was designed by Sir Thomas Bouch. He was also the designer of the ill-fated Tay Rail Bridge, swept away in a gale in December 1879 with much loss of life. It is now generally accepted that the disaster was due to a combination of exceptionally severe weather and sub-standard materials rather than any inadequacy in Bouch's design. This viaduct has stood happily for well over a century.

Continue high above the river with pleasant views of woods and farmland. The tops of the Pentland Hills peep over the trees. In 800 m pass under a bridge and into a heavily wooded cutting which leads under another bridge to Rosslyn Castle halt, where there is a picnic table on the platform.

Walk up the path by the picnic table and turn right along the road. The village of Roslin is spread out on the hill before you and there are grand views of the Pentlands. Bear right with the road and at the junction turn left on B7003. This is a busy road but there is a footpath. Directly ahead is the fang of Rosslyn Castle.

Rosslyn Chapel.

Opposite a house with the very Welsh name of Ty Gwyn, turn sharp right on a track leading down into Roslin Glen Country Park. At the river bank, turn left and follow the path along by the river to a footbridge. Cross over and continue ahead to reach steps leading steeply up to a lane. Through a gate on the right is Rosslyn Castle.

The castle, a Sinclair stronghold, dates back to the 14th century, and over its long history has suffered many indignities. Following rebuilding in 1622, it was attacked by forces under General Monk. Restored again in 1682, it was badly damaged again just six years later. In the 1980s the ruins became dangerous, but with the aid of generous government grants were made safe and partially restored to the state you see today.

After viewing the castle, return through the gate and continue up the lane. Pass the kirkyard and at the road, turn right as signed to reach Rosslyn Chapel. This is a most unexpected gem and is well worth the admission fee. Founded by Sir William Sinclair, Earl of Rosslyn, in 1446, it was intended to be a large collegiate church but was never fully completed.

It is still a very splendid building with many remarkable stone carvings on the walls and ceilings telling Bible stories. One of the 13 columns, of particular beauty, is called the Prentice Pillar and is said to have been carved by an apprentice mason while his master was away studying in Rome. When the master mason returned, he was furious to see how well his apprentice had done and in a fit of jealousy, killed him. Twenty Sinclair knights are buried in the vaults.

As you leave the chapel, notice next to it the 17th century Old Rosslyn Inn. It was a hostelry from 1660 to 1866 and its famous visitors are said to have included Dr Johnson and Boswell, Robert Burns, Sir Walter Scott and William Wordsworth.

The Prentice Pillar in Rosslyn Chapel.

Walk up the road into the village of Roslin (two pubs, shop, toilets) and turn left. In 400 m, as the road curves right, take the second turning left (with the Edinburgh Green Belt sign on the corner). Walk down this quiet lane, with more good views of the Pentlands, and go round two right-hand bends, passing the large Oatslie sand quarry on your right.

At a junction turn left, pass a new golf driving range and walk down the hill into the village of Auchendinny, with a golf course on the right. The village has a shop and the Victoria Inn. At the foot of the brae take the mill access road, and at its foot, turn right, back onto the railway path through the tunnel, to return to the starting point.

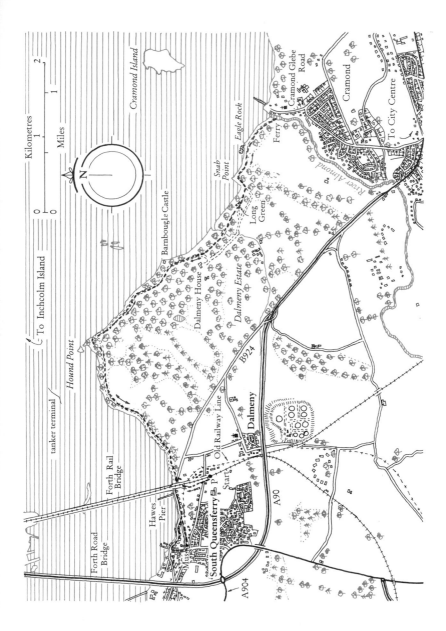

SOUTH QUEENSFERRY AND DALMENY

This delightful walk along the south shore of the Firth of Forth gives a close-up view of the two great bridges and the chance to explore South Queensferry, a historic town, and the Dalmeny Estate.

From the station car park, cross the road to a footpath which runs parallel to the railway line, towards the firth. It immediately provides an unusual view of the Road Bridge across fields. Cross the old railway line by a footbridge and at the other side, go slightly right and then down a steep flight of 120 steps known as Jacob's Ladder to the shore road.

Turn left under the railway bridge and walk into South Queensferry. There are many points of interest, only a few of which can be mentioned here. The excellent museum is well worth a visit and has a booklet telling much more of the town's history.

The Hawes Inn dates back to the late 17th century and was for centuries used by passengers travelling on the ferry to and from Fife. It features in both Stevenson's *Kidnapped* and Scott's *The Antiquary*.

Continuing into the town, you reach the Queensferry Museum on the right and then Black Castle, built in 1626. On the right, up The Vennel, is the Old Parish Kirk of 1633, and further along the High Street is the fine Tolbooth. The main part of the building dates from the 16th and early 17th centuries, but the clock tower was added in 1720 by Henry Cunningham, Member of Parliament for the area.

A short diversion to the right down Gote Lane leads to the neat wee harbour and another view of the bridges (Gote comes from a word meaning a gutter or drain). There was once a distillery here. Queensferry has had a harbour for at least 300 years, and once traded in coal, meal, timber and iron.

INFORMATION

Distance: 8 km (5 miles) one way, or 16 km (10 miles) two ways.

Start and finish: Dalmeny Station (car park).

Terrain: Roads and good tracks. No special footwear needed.

Public transport: Regular trains from Edinburgh Waverley to Dalmeny. Buses SMT 43, LRT 18 (daily), MID 47/48 (not Sundays) from city centre to South Queensferry: LRT 40/41 (not Sundays) from top of Cramond Glebe Road back to city.

Refreshments: Good selection of cafes and pubs in South Queensferry and Cramond.

Opening hours:
South Queensferry Museum: Thur-Sat 1000–1300, 1415–1700. Sun 1200–1700. Free.
Dalmeny House: May-Sep daily except Fri and Sat, 1400–1730. Admission charge.
The Cramond Ferry runs all year: Apr-Sep 0900–1900, Oct-Mar 1000–1600. Small charge.

Go left round the buildings and up to the Bellstane crossroads; note opposite Plewlands House, with its 1641 lintel. It is owned by the National Trust for Scotland. Carry on up The Loan – a name often applied in Scotland to a road to common grazings – and take the second left, Stoneycroft Road. Pass the Old School, 1671, with crowstepped gables, and continue to the end of the road at Catherine Bank, which provides an excellent view of both bridges.

Designed by Baker and Fowler, the world-famous cantilever Rail Bridge took eight years to build and in that period 56 of the 5,000 workforce lost their lives. It cost £3 million and was opened in March 1890 by the Prince of Wales (later Edward VII). The bridge contains eight million rivets and is over 2 km in length including the approaches. The track is 48 m above high water, and the tops of the towers are 100 m.

The Road Bridge opened in 1964 and was at the time the longest suspension bridge in Europe, a distinction since taken from it by several newer crossings including the Humber Bridge in England.

From the viewpoint, walk down McIvor's Brae to the shore and continue east, passing Hawes Pier, from where ferries ran to Fife until the road bridge opened in 1964. Boat trips go to the Forth islands from here in summer.

Barnbougle Castle.

Fork left, keeping by the shore and in 200 m go through a gate. The notice here actually relates to charges for the Cramond ferry and is not an attempt to make you pay for the walk! You soon see the tanker terminal off Hound Point. It is not connected to the shore as everything offloaded here is piped away.

The track gives delightful walking through the trees. Reach Hound Point, a very definite corner where the view of the Firth opens up splendidly. Inchcolm Island and the small Cramond Island are clearly seen, as is much of Edinburgh. On the left is an unexpected stretch of sandy beach which can be walked across if the tide is out.

Rejoin the track at the far end of the beach and at a main junction keep straight ahead. On the left is Barnbougle Castle, built by the 5th Earl of Rosebery (later to become Prime Minister) in 1881. Its design approximates to that of an earlier stronghold which was destroyed in 1820.

Before long, Dalmeny House appears to the right. This large Tudor Gothic mansion by William Wilkins dates from 1814 and was built for the 4th Earl of Rosebery to replace a much older house. The Roseberys have owned Dalmeny Estate for over 300 years. The house contains superb collections of furniture, tapestries, porcelain and portraits. On the lawn outside it is a large bronze statue of a horse, King Tom, by Boehm.

King Tom and Dalmeny House.

Past the house, go left as directed across the golf course to the shore, but stay inside the fence to reach a footbridge over a burn. The path continues as an avenue between trees to pass a group of estate cottages at Long Green, then climbs and swings left to give a fine view back to Barnbougle.

Once round Snab Point, the path broadens to reach Eagle Rock. The worn carving on the rock is said to have been carved by Roman legionnaires stationed at the fort at Cramond. However, as the plaque informs us, 'whether it is an eagle or whether it is even Roman is uncertain'. Ah well, it's a nice story. . . .

Shortly afterwards the path reaches the River Almond at Cramond Ferry, usually with many small boats busy here and offshore. Across the river is the causeway to Cramond Island. Your options now are to return to Dalmeny by the outward route, which is every bit as nice and gives different views westward, or to take the wee ferry across the river and, perhaps after enjoying refreshment at the inn or cafe here, walk up Cramond Glebe Road for a bus back to town.

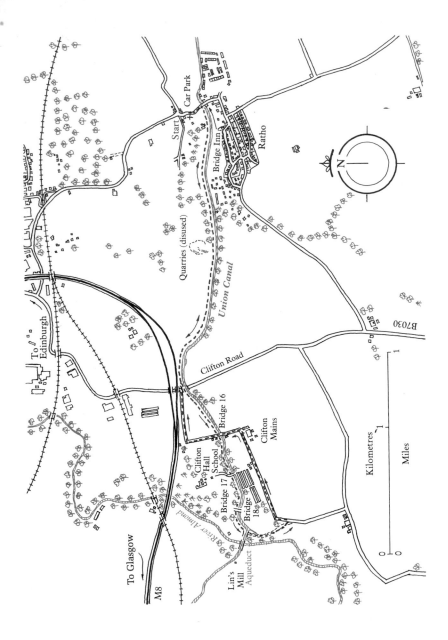

THE UNION CANAL I: RATHO TO THE ALMOND

The Union Canal west of Edinburgh still provides very pleasant and easy walking in a rural atmosphere, though it is becoming increasingly hemmed in by roads and other development. The Edinburgh & Glasgow Union Canal (its full title) originally ran for 48 km (30 miles) from the heart of Edinburgh out to Falkirk, where it stepped down a flight of locks to join the Forth & Clyde Canal as part of the original trading link with Glasgow. It carried both freight and passengers, the latter rising to some 5,000 per year in its heyday.

Work on the canal, which cost £290,000 to build, a huge amount for the time, was started in March 1818 and continued night and day until it opened in May 1822. It closed to commercial traffic in 1933, but in recent years, with a marked revival of interest in our canal heritage, many sections have been restored and are now open to pleasure boats. Trips run from Ratho (see panel for details). In late 1994, an ambitious plan to open the whole canal for navigation was announced, using money from the Millenium 2000 fund.

From the car park, walk along to the bridge and take the path down to the right to the canal towpath. The Bridge Inn and the canal cruising boats are opposite. The path wanders quietly along, passing new houses on the left after about 400 m.

INFORMATION

Distance: 9 km (5.5 miles).

Start and finish: Ratho village car park.

Terrain: Canal towpath and roads. No special footwear needed.

Public transport: ET bus 37 every two hours from St Andrew Square to Ratho.

Refreshments: Bridge Inn, Ratho.

Opening hours: *Edinburgh Canal Centre:* Open all year. For details write to the Centre at 27 Baird Road, Ratho EH28 8RA or phone 0131 333 1320. Canal trips on the *Ratho Princess* and other boats run regularly. Details from the Canal Centre or the Bridge Inn.

Cruise boats at Ratho.

The canal then enters a wooded section with tall trees to either side, pleasantly shady in summer and busy with birdsong. Enjoy the peace and quiet of this wooded section: things are soon to change dramatically. As the woods end, there is a rumbling off to the right. The rumbling becomes a roar and the M8 motorway appears, almost within touching distance. The canal narrows for the bridge over Clifton Road, then resumes its former width and swings leftward. As you continue along this stretch, the motorway happily removes itself to a sensible distance, a relief for the eardrums.

Pass under bridge 16, the first of three reached in short order, with neat houses to either side. The narrowboat *Thomas Telford* has been seen moored on this section: very appropriate, as the great engineer was much involved in canal work, the Caledonian Canal being perhaps the apotheosis of his career.

Bridge 17 is a splendid high arch, now in the grounds of Clifton Hall School. Shortly afterwards you pass under bridge 18, and you must now prepare yourself for another surprise and delight. The valley of the River Almond lies ahead, and with the confidence typical of its time, the canal vaults over it on a magnificent 1821 aqueduct. This is the highest structure of its type in Scotland, standing 39m above the valley floor, and the third highest in Britain (Telford's Pontcysyllte in Wales is tops).

The magnificent Almond Aqueduct.

There is a small basin beside the aqueduct, with a car parking and picnic area. The boats cruising from Ratho can be seen turning here, after they have given their passengers a brief sensation of flying by going back and forth on the aqueduct. There is nothing new in this: an 1834 handbill for the canal offered a trip of ten miles (16 km) for sixpence (2½p), 'amidst most pleasant scenery and over highly interesting aqueducts, at one of which fruits, confectioneries and varieties of refreshments can be had'.

There are no fruits or confectioneries on sale here today, but you can still marvel at the highly interesting aqueduct. After walking across, enjoying the views up and down river, and walking back again, go left down a long flight of steps to see the aqueduct from below. Pass underneath the great brick arches, which look as sound now as they would have done when new 170 years ago, and walk up the lane to start the return journey. The aqueduct is partly obscured by trees but its strength and size is still apparent. Beyond it is Lin's Mill, where William I in was the last man in Scotland to die of the plague, in 1645.

At the top of the lane, join a road and go straight ahead. Go 90 degrees left with the road at Clifton Mains and cross the canal. The pretty Victoria Cottage here has an 1874 datestone - and a fine view of the canal. The motorway draws near again. Go right with the road at the entrance to Clifton Hall (where a notice proclaims that the school caters for both boarders and day pupils of both sexes aged from 3 to 13½) and walk along beside the M8.

At the road junction go straight over and up a rough track to rejoin the canal towpath for the 2 km walk back through the trees to Ratho. It is very much worth looking at Ratho Church, which dates from the 16th century. Among the graves in the kirkyard is a coffin-shaped memorial to one William Mitchell, farmer, who suffered 'an instantaneous death from a stroke by a threshing machine, December 1800'. Clearly a local tragedy from 200 years ago long remembered.

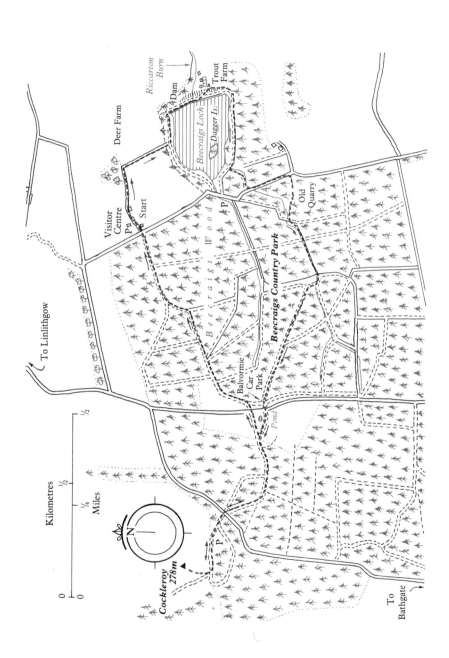

Riccarton Burn

Trout Farm

Deer Farm

Dam

Beecraigs Loch

Dagger Is.

Visitor Centre

Start

B e e c r a i g s   W o o d

Beecraigs Country Park

Old Quarry

To Linlithgow

Balvormie Car Park

Pond

Kilometres

Miles

N

Cockleroy 278m

To Bathgate

BEECRAIGS AND COCKLEROY

Beecraigs, the largest country park in West Lothian, covers nearly 300 ha, much of it woodland, in the Bathgate Hills south of Linlithgow. The park sits among a maze of small lanes and it is not difficult to miss the right entrance. There are several car parks, all marked on our map, and if you do go wrong the walk can be joined at any of them.

The park offers a wide variety of outdoor activities, from field archery to sailing, and has a 'trim course', climbing net and other facilities. Details are available at the visitor centre, which has good displays, leaflets and information on wildlife.

From the corner of the visitor centre car park, take the signposted deer walkway through part of the deer farm. A large herd of red deer is kept at Beecraigs and farmed for venison. It gives an opportunity to see Britain's largest mammal at quite close quarters. In September and October you may hear the stags bellowing their rutting call as the mating season is reached.

INFORMATION

Distance: 8 km (5 miles).

Start/finish: Beecraigs Country Park Visitor Centre, 3 km south of Linlithgow at GR 007747. Best found by following signs from Linlithgow to the country park and then to Beecraigs Restaurant. Turn off past the restaurant and the visitor centre car park is 400 m further on, on the left.

Terrain: Paths and tracks which can be muddy in places. Strong footwear recommended.

Public transport: None to park. Nearest either Linlithgow (train or bus) or Torphichen (bus).

Refreshments: Shop at visitor centre selling drinks and snacks. Beecraigs restaurant (licensed, meals). Wide selection in Linlithgow.

Opening hours: Beecraigs Visitor Centre: Apr-Sep Mon-Thur 0900–1700, Fri 0900–1600, Sat 1300–1800, Sun 1000–1800. Oct-Mar Mon-Thur 0900–1700, Fri 0900–1600, Sat closed, Sun 1100–1600. Tel: 01506 844516.

Linlithgow Palace from Cockleroy.

Turn right with the path – the two great bridges are visible away to the left – and then leave the deer farm to go into the woods. Turn left along by Beecraigs Loch. Just along here is a notice about a badger sett which can be seen in the trees, but unless you come at dusk you are most unlikely to catch sight of these lovely animals.

Turn right onto the dam, and take the steps on the left down to the trout farm. You can buy a bag of food for a small sum and watch the trout leap as you scatter it on the water. In one of the ponds is an amusing sea monster sculpture, apparently rising out of the water to drag you under. Opposite it a very realistic carved heron waits motionless for food. Delicious trout is on sale at the visitor centre or you can really spoil your cat by buying it a bag of offcuts!

From the trout farm, continue on the road round the loch, passing Dagger Island. Cross a small bridge and turn left onto a path (red arrow). Walk alongside the burn for a while, then cross the burn as directed and walk beside the road for 200 m before crossing.

Continue on the path. To the left is an old quarry which has a climbing wall. There are many paths and tracks in this part of the park so directions need to be followed reasonably carefully. Cross two footbridges and continue through the pinewoods. Join another path and go half left, still following red arrows.

At a cross path (a pony route) go straight on. Cross an old dyke and reach a wider track (signed as an ATB route). Go straight ahead. In about 400 m another track joins it from the left. Keep ahead and reach a road at the Balvormie car park.

Cross the road and walk left of a small pond, pass the barbecue area and walk over to the right to the toilets. Turn left along the track passing in front of the toilets. It can be quite muddy here. Swing right with a blue arrow.

Start counting these arrows, pointing back the way. At the third arrow in about 400 m from the toilets, turn right on a smaller path that winds through the trees, partly on duckboards. At another junction in 300 m turn left to reach a road. Cross the road, pass left of a small car park, and continue on the path now signed to Cockleroy.

The path runs alongside a stone dyke. In 250 m reach a stile on the right and cross it; there is a notice stating that Cockleroy is private ground and asking you to keep dogs strictly under control and to take the most direct route to the summit. The hill rears up ahead but the top is easily enough gained if you take it steadily.

Beecraigs Loch.

The reward for the climb is great. Small hill, big view. The panorama extends across most of Central Scotland, it seems, with most of the principal landmarks marked on an indicator erected by the AA in 1980. It points rather optimistically to Goat Fell on Arran (106 km away) and Ben Lomond (69 km), but in good conditions you still command a stupendous prospect.

Below you to the north is Linlithgow with its palace and loch. Beyond is the broad Forth, the Fife and Ochil Hills, the chimneys and lights of Grangemouth, and in the other direction the Pentlands. It's a great place to pause, admire what you see and take some photographs. I once came up here in a mist so thick I had to leave little markers on the climb to avoid getting lost on the way back – not recommended!

When you are ready to return, retrace your steps to the stile, then back through the wood to the road and across all the way to the Balvormie car park. Cross the car park and at its far lefthand corner take a path then a broad track, passing the big climbing net which may tempt younger walkers.

The track leads back directly to the road at the entrance to the visitor centre car park. Perhaps you'll choose to take some venison or trout home with you. On one visit, a friend and I were entertained on the walk back from Balvormie by a three-year-old called Michaela out with her grandparents. On reaching the visitor centre, she told us with scorn that under the table was a 'kid-on deer'. I swear the poor stuffed animal drooped its eyes in shame!

Linlithgow Loch and the Palace.

Cormorant

200 m to reach an open area. Cross it and go left and then right, behind new houses, into a lane.

At the entry to Lochmill Lodge go left and continue between fences for 300 m to reach St Ninian's Road. Cross the road, go left and in 15 m right on the path leading to Linlithgow Loch. If you wish to shorten the walk a little, go right here and walk round the loch to the Palace. For the full walk, go left and walk along the north shore of the loch, with the noisy M9 almost beside you.

The compensation is the varied birdlife and the splendid views across to the Palace on its knoll. The loch, which extends to 40 ha, is a designated Site of Special Scientific Interest. Among the 90 species of birds recorded here are swans, goldeneye, grebes and cormorants. The small island is called The Rickle.

At the north-east end of the loch, go right and walk down its east side, passing Hatchery Bay and Cormorant Island and crossing the Bonnytoun Burn. The yellow water lilies at the south-east corner are said to have been flourishing here for over 400 years. From here you need to exit to Blackness Road. Turn right along the road until a lane gives access past St Michael's Catholic Church to the lochside again.

The Palace.

The Palace stands on its mound, called The Peel. The present building dates from the mid 15th century. Building continued for some time, but by the time Mary, Queen of Scots was born here on 8 December 1542, the Palace would have been much as we see it today. After the Union of the Crowns in 1603 the Palace was much less used, and Charles I was the last monarch to sleep here, in July 1633.

The Palace was held by Cromwell's forces from 1650 until 1659. Bonnie Prince Charlie was here in 1745 and the following year, while occupied by the Duke of Cumberland's troops, the Palace was seriously damaged by fire and was never rebuilt. It has been maintained as an ancient monument since 1874 and a walk around this still splendid building, redolent with Scottish history, makes a marvellous climax to the walk.

Bonnie Prince Charlie

Next to the Palace is St Michael's Church. Originally dedicated in 1242, much of the existing building dates from the 15th century. It has fine stained glass, and its aluminium 'crown of thorns', designed by Geoffrey Clarke and completed in 1964, is a very prominent landmark.

INDEX